Especially for Ministers' Wives

Especially for Ministers' Wives

125 Ideas
on
**Parsonage Management • Interior Decorating
Entertaining • Showers • Family Worship
Budgeting • Gift Ideas
Outreach Projects • Meditations**

Compiled by

Bonnie McGraw Wiseman

Beacon Hill Press of Kansas City
Kansas City, Missouri

Copyright, 1978
Beacon Hill Press of Kansas City

ISBN: 0-8341-0553-5

Printed in the
United States of America

Permission to quote from the following copyrighted versions of the Bible is acknowledged with appreciation.

The Living Bible (TLB), © 1971 by Tyndale House Publishers, Wheaton, Ill.

New American Standard Bible (NASB), © The Lockman Foundation, 1960, 1962, 1968, 1971, 1972, 1973, 1975.

New International Version of the New Testament (NIV), © 1973 by the New York Bible Society International.

Contents

Preface   9

Parsonage Management   11

    20 Ideas for Making Housework Easier *(Pat Morsch)*
    My "To Do" List *(Janice Tyler)*
    Details About My Guests *(Evelyn DeVore)*
    Planned Freezer Meals *(Betty Lynch)*
    Those Dreadful Oven Racks *(Chris Grauman)*
    Cook Ahead *(Helen Leeper)*
    Time with Parsonage Children *(Ruby Vogt)*
    Planning Menus for Evangelists *(Kathryn Richey)*
    Samoan Lessons *(Polly Appleby)*
    Nine Time-Management Rules *(Myrna Hazlett)*
    Time-Management Idea *(Pat Freeland)*
    Navy Lessons *(Patty Dobbs)*
    Household Ideas *(Dakota Ministers' Wives)*

Interior Decorating   27

    Decorating for Christmas *(Marsha Crouch)*
    Bathroom Curtains *(Barbara Chaney)*
    Dried Flower Bouquets *(Louise Wert)*
    Borrowed Paintings *(Jeannette Iglesias)*
    Bathroom Decorating *(Phyllis Briscoe)*
    A Bible Story Quilt *(Jo Ann Fustin)*
    Oil Finish on Refinished Furniture *(Sue Duncan)*
    Give Each Parsonage Your Unique Touch
       (Paulette Woods)
    Antiquing *(Betty Fruehling)*
    Picture Grouping *(Martha Liner)*
    Bathroom Accessories *(Marie Ray)*
    Hanging Tips *(Donna Martin)*
    10 Decorating Rules *(Vera Rushford)*

Entertaining   38

    Joyful Entertaining *(Joyce Thompson)*
    Dressed Up Lemons *(Clarice Moore)*

Double Duty Hospitality *(Wilma Peters)*
Balloon Party Invitations *(Vonnie Savage)*
Special Cobbler Decorations *(Vonnie Savage)*
KISS System *(Ruth Patton)*
Sunday Night Buffet *(Betty Lynch)*
Monthly Anniversary Reception *(Ruby Heap)*
Swap Luncheon *(Paulette Woods)*
Appetizers Make Entertaining Easier *(Cheryl Roland)*
Entertaining Special Speakers *(Evelyn Vandervort)*
Children Help Serve Dinner *(Joan Bottles)*
Songs for Mother-Daughter Banquet *(Twila Umbel)*
Christmas with Your Church Families *(Betty Hoose)*
Mother-Son Breakfast *(Geneva Fetters)*
Ladies' Day Out *(Judi Grimshaw)*

Shower Ideas 52

"I Predict . . ." *(Rosamond Max)*
Practical Corsages *(Ruth Killen)*
Popcorn Cake Centerpiece *(Shirley Belzer)*
Decorated Candles *(Mae Bahan)*
Bridal Shower Fun *(Twila Umbel)*
Mother's Frozen Food Shower *(Barbara Boone)*
Pacifier Mints *(Jan Stetson)*
No. 2 Baby Shower *(Jadene Payton)*
Bride and Groom Shower *(Glinda Williams)*
Baby Shower Centerpiece *(Phillis Dickinson)*

Family Worship 61

Weekly Family Scripture *(Barbara Chaney)*
Easy Bible Memorization *(Jadene Payton)*
Genesis Game *(Cheryl Roland)*
Story Book for Devotions *(Jadene Payton)*
Devotional Planning by Children *(Anita Ulrich)*
Developing Children's Interest in Devotions
    (Wilma Shaw)
Handmade Scrolls for Family Devotions
    (Thelma Locke)
A Christmas Puppet Devotional *(Clarice Swift)*
Use Children's Reading Skills *(Sheila DeMott)*
Worship for a Hyperactive Child *(Joyce MacMillan)*

Your Happiest Moment? *(Wanda Matthews)*
In the Morning *(Sue Kinzler)*
A Memory Board *(Lola Daniels)*
Traps Are to Stay Out Of *(Carol Pounds)*

Living on a Shoestring Budget 73

Six Rules for Stretching the Budget *(Mae Bahan)*
Vegetable Centerpiece *(Barbara Chaney)*
Now Hear Ye This *(Lola Williams)*
Making Dresses Do Triple Duty *(Pauline Spray)*
Shoestring Shopping and Eating *(Paulette Woods)*
A Christmas Card Design *(Rachel Ellis)*
Gourmet TV Dinners *(Maudie Clack)*
How to Budget *(Myrna Hazlett)*
Recipe for Hungry Teens *(Doris Restrick)*
Double-Knit Thrift *(Joan Whittenberger)*
A Bridal Attendant's Headpice *(Pauline Spray)*
Drapes and Tablecloths from Sheets
    (Barbara Chaney)
Budgeting *(Sandra Felter)*
Inexpensive Tablecloths *(Barbara Chaney)*
Instant Stuffing *(Shirley Reed)*
Guidelines for Shopping *(Lynn Bledsaw)*

Inexpensive Gifts 85

Decoupage Announcements *(Sue Prentice)*
Gifts for the Church Board *(Sheila DeMott)*
Thank-you Gift for VBS Workers *(Ann Cannon)*
Lambs for Newborns *(Joan Whittenberger)*
Place Mats and Napkins *(Jo Ann Fustin)*
Handmade Wooden Puzzles *(Marsha Crouch)*
Baby Jar Gifts *(Mary Winkle)*
Emergency Purse Kit *(Ella Martin)*
Washcloth and Guest Towel Holder
    (Anna Marie Lockard)
Memory Box *(Joan Whittenberger)*
The Gift Shelf *(Name Withheld)*
Christmas Ornament Gifts *(Carolyn Wade)*
A Gift of Inspiring Scripture *(Virginia Lord)*
Green Plant and Strawberry Box *(Joan Stewart)*

Unique Outreach 98
    City Hall Bible Studies *(Wilma Utter)*
    Pastry Evangelism *(Ramona Cone)*
    Stop and Go Appreciation *(Chris Blankenship)*
    Post Office Thank-you *(Carolyn Davis)*
    A Friendship or Prayer Partner Tea
        (Eleanor Sullivan)
    Lunch Box Fellowship *(Elaine Cunningham)*
    Cradle Roll Outreach *(Gladys Hurt)*
    A Ladies' Slumber Party *(Carolyn Ireland)*
    Bible Clubs *(Virginia Dace)*
    Outreach by the Loaf *(Doris Restrick)*
    Love Breakfast *(Nancy Scharler)*
    A Ministry of Mail *(Arlene Mottram)*
    Christmas Outreach *(Adele Storkson)*
    Fashion Festival *(Diane Jones)*
    Community Involvement *(Yvonne Chalfant)*

Meditations for Women's Meetings 111
    From Darkness to Light *(Emily Moore)*
    Thoughts of a Mother *(Rosalyn Appleby)*
    Garth's God *(Joan Whittenberger)*
    The First Step *(Barbara Borgal)*
    Independent Darla *(Pauline Spray)*
    What Do You See? *(Ruth Patton)*
    Furnace or Faith *(Karen Wylie)*
    Cease Useless Striving *(Emmelyne Helsel)*
    Baby Chicks and God's Love *(Guynell Mullis)*
    31 Days to a New Prayer Life *(Elizabeth Wyss)*
    Roses and Storms *(Lynn Taylor)*
    Shepherd of My Life *(Jeannette Shows)*
    "How?" Not "Why?" *(Kathryn Johnson)*
    Have You Seen Them? *(Carolyn Cordell)*
    If You Love People, Tell Them *(Linnea Oke)*
    We Are His Responsibility *(Ida Mae Mickey)*

Preface

Go to any meeting of ministers' wives and you soon discover that parsonage women come in different sizes, ages, and perspectives. But the God who created every snowflake different and every maple leaf unique delights in such diversity.

WILCON, a series of Leadership Conferences for Nazarene ministers' wives, brought this book into existence. More than 5,000 ministers' wives were asked to submit insightful ways of sharing ministry with their preacher-husbands. The overwhelming response has me embarrassed by the fact that space limitations kept us from printing nearly 200 submitted ideas.

This book provides new ideas for the veteran parsonage ladies. Beginners will find help here, too. For every parsonage lady there is encouragement that a lot of ministers' wives are finding satisfaction in Kingdom service.

The fulfillment I have enjoyed in organizing this book has reminded me that my roots make me a third generation Nazarene minister's wife. My grandmothers on both sides of the family significantly shared a pioneer home mission ministry with my grandfathers. My mother married an oil company accountant who answered a call to the ministry while both were in their late 20s. And my preacher-husband has been pastor, college chaplain, professor, editor, writer, and now denominational director of ministerial development. Thus, I have been close to the spiritual action by living in parsonages most of my life. And it is fun.

—BONNIE McGRAW WISEMAN

I

Parsonage Management

20 Ideas for Making Housework Easier

This is not an orginal idea but it is a list of ways I have found to be very useful in making my housework a little easier.

1. Write it down: shopping errands, people to call, home projects, appointments, and odd jobs to be done.
2. Set up a message center in a convenient, visible place for pinning up reminders, notes, family messages, and who-should-do-what-when.
3. Keep a small notebook in your purse for jotting

down clothing sizes you need to know, birthdays and anniversaries, and phone numbers.

4. Limit your food shopping, except for specialities, to one good, convenient market.

5. Put your shopping list in the same order as the store aisles to save steps.

6. Double-check recipes, and your shelves, for ingredients you may be missing.

7. Check off items on your list as you fill your shopping cart. Do not shop when you are hungry.

8. Avoid shopping during store's busiest hours.

9. Avoid shopping with small children.

10. Streamline your housekeeping and reexamine your standards. Don't be a perfectionist. Weed out unnecessary jobs and time-wasting habits.

11. Use wax to save work on window sills, kitchen cabinets, appliances, and light switch areas. This protects surfaces and makes dirt easier to remove.

12. Vacuum before you dust.

13. Keep cleaning aids efficient: cloths and mops clean, vacuum cleaner filter bags changed, air filters clean.

14. Use quilts as bedcovers. They are popular and decorative.

15. Use sheets of different colors on each bed for instant sorting after laundering.

16. Dovetail errands and their locations.

17. Shop and bank by mail.

18. Plan menus in advance but keep plans flexible.

19. Eliminate washday. Do a load a day.

20. Group items on a refrigerator or cabinet shelf that almost always go on the table for a particular meal (such

as butter, jelly, jam, cream, milk, and sugar for breakfast) to save trips.

Mrs. J. V. (Pat) Morsch
Orlando, Florida

My "To Do" List

Place all duties, projects, and pleasures into specific time slots. Keep a mental "list" of long-range plans, and definite pencil-and-paper lists for shorter-range plans. The "loosest" list includes things needing to be done in the next three months. From that, make a day-by-day schedule for the coming month. The real "working list" is for the coming week. On this, chart hour-by-hour schedules along with meal plans. As things are done, cross them off. One may be completely changed by emergency; another may go so well jobs can be "borrowed" from the future or caught up from the past. Some tasks might be forgotten completely if not written down for a specific time slot. Having meals planned by the week makes grocery shopping easier—saves money too.

Time budgeting relieves some of the stress of worrying about many things at once. After writing a duty on paper and planning sufficient time to do it, forget it and concentrate on more urgent duties.

Mrs. Donald E. (Janice) Tyler
Ottawa, Illinois

Details About My Guests

I keep a 3 x 5 card file about our visitors. On this card I type the names of the Mr. and Mrs., and the members of the family. If this family returns, you immediately have names you can ask about. People always like to have someone ask about their children or grandchildren. You can pick up this information just by listening during their first visit in your home. Add birthdays and anniversaries; it is such a surprise for them to receive a card from you during the year. This is especially a great idea for missionaries and their children who have visited your home and church.

On this card you can record the likes and dislikes of foods. Many people have diets; everyone has a few choice foods they especially like. If they have certain times of the day they prefer to eat, note that. If they like to fast a meal, remember that, too.

In this file you may want to keep record of each family or group you entertain, what is served, and so on. This keeps you from serving the same food to them next time.

Mrs. Elvin (Evelyn) DeVore
Denver, Colorado

Planned Freezer Meals

Unexpected company arrives about an hour before mealtime. Let's go out. That may be the solution you would like, but it is so expensive, and even our denominational leaders tell us that they appreciate a good home-cooked meal.

Plan ahead and freeze food for those family members or friends who drop by unexpectedly.

If a chicken is cleaned before freezing, it can be placed in a Corning Ware dish, covered with barbeque sauce, and can be baked in the oven in one hour and 15 minutes. Put in potatoes to bake. Then add canned vegetables.

Cakes or pies can be prepared, wrapped and frozen, ready to serve. Or freeze an angel food cake. Take it out, slice it horizontally twice and separate to thaw. Whip a package of Dream Whip topping. Make a package of instant pudding (any flavor), mix with the Dream Whip, and alternate layers of this with your cake. Cover the outside of the cake with the remainder. This makes a lovely torte.

I always keep bacon and coffee cake or cinnamon rolls frozen, ready for unexpected breakfasts. If the bacon does not have time to thaw, place it in your broiler. Set on 450°. As it thaws, separate the slices. It will be done by the time everything else is ready.

For variety with meat, prepare a ready-to-bake meatloaf and freeze. Prepare hamburger patties and freeze with a piece of foil between each.

If you do not have a freezer, keep one shelf of the cabinet stocked "for company use only." Use canned meats. Plan a cookie-crust pie with instant pie filling.

MRS. W. M. (BETTY) LYNCH
Richardson, Texas

Those Dreadful Oven Racks

Tired of the torture and time it takes to clean your oven racks? Or maybe you cannot stand the raw hands and sore arms from scrubbing and scouring to have a sparkling oven? Relax, and use your time more meaningfully.

Remove anything removeable from your oven (racks,

broiler pan, rack guides, bottom drip sheet). Place them all in the bathtub. Run as hot water as possible to cover all the paraphernalia and pour in 1½ to 2 cups of regular ammonia.

When racks have soaked for six hours or more, drain out the ammonia water to avoid burning your hands on the chemical. Re-cover the racks with tepid water. Now, all you need to do is scrub lightly with a pot scrubber or brush and the baked-on grease and grime will literally float away. Before placing the dried racks back on the oven, spray lightly with Pam or Cooking Ease to facilitate cleaning the next time.

One caution: do not use this method on aluminum burner drip pans, as they will discolor from the ammonia.

MRS. RONALD L. (CHRIS) GRAUMAN
Dwight, Illinois

Cook Ahead

After putting away the groceries, I like to fry my ground beef (2 or 3 pounds) with chopped onion and seasoning. Chop it with a fork or spatula as it fries. Drain and place in Corning Ware casserole. When cool, store in freezer until ready to use. An ice pick will chip off enough for pizzas, spaghetti sauce, or sloppy joes, and the remainder can be put back in the freezer.

Likewise, I place my roast, a can of mushrooms, and chopped onions in the Crock Pot for about six hours. When cooked, make the gravy by heating "pot juice," mushrooms, and onions, and adding flour and water mixture. Pour over medium-thin sliced roast. When cool, place in freezer. It will be a lifesaver some Sunday when you do not feel like cooking. Just take out to thaw before going to church, and place in the oven for about 30 minutes after church.

> Mrs. Lawrence E. (Helen) Leeper
> *Orlando, Florida*

Time with Parsonage Children

"I hope I can find a place to work where I can be at home with my family as much as my dad was with us." That statement, made by our oldest son after graduation from law school, totally surprised and amazed me for I knew that my pastor-husband was gone from home a lot in the course of shepherding the church flocks and serving on various district boards and committees.

Reflecting on his comment, I recalled that as our boys were growing up, we tried to spend one evening per week with them during the school months, and one day per week during the summertime. We made candy, popped popcorn, played table games, went on picnics, and other things that they liked to do. I believe the secret was that this one evening or that one day per week was totally for them and so it seemed that their dad was with them a lot, simply because he gave them his whole attention for that period of time. Even if one evening or a whole day is not available, one hour of undivided attention in a young child's life will seem like a long time. The quantity of time was not the big thing, but the quality of it was what made the deep impression on their lives.

No, I have never told our son that his dad was gone a lot. His memory of those fun times is more important than any correction of the amount of time spent.

I firmly believe that this had some bearing on the fact that both of our sons are Christians today and active in their local churches.

Mrs. Kenneth (Ruby) Vogt
Renton, Washington

Planning Menus for Evangelists

Plan meals ahead.

Write out menus for entire time company will be there.

Plan a day at a time (breakfast, lunch, dinner, and snack) so that you will have a well-balanced combination. If you are having a steak or roast for dinner, be sure to plan a lighter lunch, like a salad. Each meal should be nutritious, tasty, and attractive. Think of color combinations when planning vegetables and salads.

Buy ahead.

Watch for your best buys on top quality meats, ice cream, and other items which can be frozen. Also watch for sales on top brands of canned goods.

Bake ahead.

For example, you can bake a variety of cookies that will help vary desserts.

Buy in-season foods whenever possible.

In-season foods are fresher and usually less expensive.

Do not waste good food.

Freeze leftovers immediately following the meal. Most

meats, vegetables, and desserts can be frozen. They will taste great after your company is gone, and the work of preparing is already done.

Keep your menus on file for future reference.

Enjoy entertaining.

MRS. MYRON E. (KATHRYN) RICHEY
West Grove, Pennsylvania

Samoan Lessons

Early in our ministry, while serving in the beautiful Samoan Islands, my husband and I felt a definite need to budget our time. The leisurely pace did not lend us needed inspiration to be organized. But God did not let us sit around squeezing sand between our sunbaked toes. He gave us a plan that we have continued to this day.

Early in the week we set a time for a regular weekly meeting. We kept good minutes. Everything was listed that needed to be done that week. The list might include families to be visited, letters to be written, a porch painted, and a clinic visit. In a few weeks we were happily surprised at the results.

Now pastoring in Hawaii, we continue our meetings with the ministerial staff and their wives. At our Thursday luncheon we each take a list of things we want to do that week. It is so satisfying to be able to check off items as they are accomplished.

It is amazing what God can do through you when you carefully control your time.

MRS. JERRY L. (POLLY) APPLEBY
Honolulu, Hawaii

Nine Time-Management Rules

1. Have certain days to do weekly tasks.
2. Pick up after the children go to bed so you can get up to a partly straightened house.
3. Get up a half hour before the family so you can have your devotions.
4. Complete one task before starting another.
5. Always have beds made, dishes done, and odds and ends picked up; then nobody will notice a little dust.
6. If you are going to have a very busy day, put your evening meal in your slow cooker so your family will be in good spirits at mealtime.
7. Plan your meals for the week so you have fewer trips to the store; you will have variety, and it costs less if you plan.
8. Do not make your husband late.
9. Take time for yourself.

MRS. G. A. (MYRNA) HAZLETT
Warren, Ohio

Time-Management Idea

I utilize my time at the beauty shop by writing letters, reading missionary books, crocheting, addressing newsletters, etc. Some things can also be done while riding in the car.

MRS. RON (PAT) FREELAND
Petersburg, Indiana

Navy Lessons

When my husband first went into the navy I read *The Navy Officers' Wives' Manual,* and one idea has helped me for many years. It is to spend three minutes just before retiring at night to tidy the living area, fluff sofa pillows, straighten magazines, put up misplaced articles, rinse dessert dishes and stack neatly in the sink. You always enjoy the morning just a bit better and could even enjoy an early caller.

Mrs. Don (Patty) Dobbs
Penticton, British Columbia, Canada

Household Ideas

Felt-tip Markers

Store felt-tipped markers in a sealed jar to keep them from drying out. This is especially important if you have some with lost caps.

Cut Flowers

A thin slice of mild soap put into the water with cut flowers will keep them fresh longer.

House Plants

Sponge leaves of house plants with milk to remove dust and give the foliage luster.

Sticking Doors

For a door that rubs against the floor, lay a piece of

course sandpaper rough side up on the floor and swing the door across it several times until it moves freely.

Salt

It is important how and when you add salt in cooking. To blend with soups and sauces, put it in early; add to meats just before taking from the stove. In cake ingredients, salt can be mixed with the eggs. When cooking vegetables, always salt the water in which they are cooked. Put salt in the pan when frying fish.

Deodorizer

Leave a bottle of lemon juice uncorked in bathroom—it is a good deodorizer.

Heartburn

Did you know that raw potatoes are great for relief of heartburn?

Gum Removal

To remove chewing gum from a carpet or a child's hair, rub the gum with ice to harden and scrape off.

Biscuit Cutter

Use divider from an ice tray to cut biscuits in hurry. Shape dough to conform with size of divider and cut. After baking, biscuits will separate at dividing line.

African Violets

To prevent African violet leaves from touching the pot edges, slit a lace-paper doily, remove the center and fit it under the leaves like a collar.

Quick Baked Potatoes

Make a solution using 1¼ cups salt to 2 qts. water. Boil potatoes in this for 20 minutes. Remove from water, rinse in hot water. Bake in 450 degree oven for 5 minutes or place under the broiler. Serve with butter or sour cream.

Eggs

To keep eggs from cracking, put a small hole in one end of the egg with a straight pin before cooking.

Crackers

If you have stale crackers or potato chips—put them in a pan and heat in a 250 degree oven for 5 or 10 minutes.

Pizza

When rolling out pizza dough, put flour on hands instead of shortening.

Windows

Quick and inexpensive way to wash windows: Use vinegar in water and wash, then shine dry with wadded up newspaper. Leaves no lint and really shines.

Pot Cleaner

To clean stainless steel pots and pans, use newspaper with scouring powders. It takes away stains and the pans shine beautifully.

Egg Subtitute

If you are short on eggs, use ¼ cup of baking powder in your cake.

Porcelain Stains

Use lemon juice or vinegar to remove the rust stains from your bathroom porcelain caused by leaking faucets.

Tulips

To prolong the life of cut tulips, put a few pennies in bottom of the vase.

Silverware

To remove black spots on silverware, drop a little machine oil on each spot, rub, then polish as usual.

Furniture Spots

To remove white spots and rings on furniture, cover with cotton soaked in iodine and then rub.

Candle Wax

To remove candle wax from fabric, scrape as much as possible from the surface with a dull blade. Then cover the stain on both sides with blotting paper and press with a hot iron. Follow this by laundering in cold water.

Pictures

To keep pictures hanging straight, paste a small piece of sandpaper on the back of the picture near the bottom.

Fires

Ordinary baking soda can be used to extinguish small fires quickly.

Sweater Storage

To keep sweaters nice and save drawer space, fold

shoulder to shoulder and roll. Lay side by side in drawer. Each sweater is in full view and is never wrinkled.

Chrysanthemums

A little sugar added to the water of cut chrysanthemums will help them stay fresh.

Raisins

Before adding raisins to the batter for cakes or muffins, heat them in a dish over low heat or hot water until they are very warm. This will prevent them from sinking to the bottom of the cake or muffin.

Syrup

Before measuring syrup, honey, or molasses, grease the measuring cup or spoon with butter to prevent the syrup from clining to cup or spoon.

Steam

To avoid steaming up the entire bathroom, run cool water in tub first then add the hot.

Candles

A good use for candle stubs is to melt them down over low heat and add spices or a few whole cloves. Pour into attractive molds with wicks and use for air freshening in bathrooms and other places.

Funnels

Paint an old funnel and make an attractive, useful twine holder for the kitchen.

Organize Freezer

Freeze vegetables or other foods in square plastic containers. When the food is frozen, take out and place in plastic bags. Then pack the plastic bags into half gallon milk cartons. Saves space.

Onions

Onions dipped in scalding water before peeling will never cause the eyes to water. To remove onion smell from hands, place a stainless steel knife between your thumb and fingers and rub under cold water.

Electric Cords

For neat storage of appliance cords, fold cords in 12-inch lengths and insert in paper towel cardboard tubes.

MINISTERS' WIVES
Dakota District

2

Interior Decorating

Decorating for Christmas

For coordinated Christmas decorations that can be used throughout the house, buy 10 yards of a red, white, and green plaid cotton and make the following items: a runner for the top of the piano; a padded cover for the piano bench; a runner for the table; round tablecloths for end tables; a floor-length tablecloth for "open house"; a wrap and a large bow for an egg-shaped plant holder; bows for the drapery tiebacks; a tree skirt; a large, braided wreath for the front door; and a variety of ornaments for the tree. Use some of the material scraps and make some patchwork throw pillows. Quilting is "in." Since these items will be used one month out of the year, they will last for several Christmas seasons.

MRS. ORBIN N. (MARSHA) CROUCH
Custer City, Oklahoma

Bathroom Curtains

Bathroom curtains can take shape in a hurry after a move. Use cafe curtain rods with matching towels at windows. Many use these all the time, changing pattern or solid color when desired. They are easy to keep clean, and quick to design.

MRS. REEFORD L. (BARBARA) CHANEY
Richmond, Virginia

Dried Flower Bouquets

Bouquets of lasting beauty are yours for the picking. Gather dried wild flowers and grasses in the fall for autumn and winter decorating. For added color, spray flowers lightly with spray paint. To remove excess fluff, spray flowers with a fixative from any art supply store. The following is a list of wild flowers and grasses that can be found over most of America.

- Baby's breath—has dainty white blossoms
- Common mullein—bright yellow, dry to dark brown
- Sensitive fern—large lobed fern leaves
- Steeplebush—tiny pink flowers, form cones of reddish brown
- Wild oats—one of many wild grasses found in all fields

- Horsemint—flower forms clusters of seedpods
- Teasel—tiny lavender flowers
- Goldenrod—dries well; shake off excess fluff, spray with fixative
- Milkweed—common plant that always looks good in its common state
- Yarrow—flat clusters of white and pink flowers
- Queen Anne's lace—flat white clusters that curl up in fall
- Seedbox—pods are light brown color
- Cattail—should be gathered before they burst and dipped in shellac
- Coneflower—flower heads dry naturally

MRS. RALPH E. (LOUISE) WEST
Alexandria, Louisiana

Borrowed Paintings

Your public library may be the answer to part of your home decorating needs. Many libraries have reproductions of famous paintings that may be borrowed on your library card. The appearance of rooms can be changed with no cost involved. A "Renoir" hanging in the parsonage living room can do wonders for the atmosphere. When the snows are knee-deep in the winter, enjoy a bright painting filled with yellow flowers in the kitchen. It is fun to be able to satisfy the desire for a change in an economical way.

MRS. DAVID (JEANNETTE) IGLESIAS
Washington, New Jersey

Bathroom Decorating

Some inexpensive ideas in bathroom decorating are as follows:

For the shower/bathtub area, take two matching twin flat sheets in prints, plaids, stripes, or solids; preferably with contrasting color hems. Measure the width of the opening for your shower curtain, allowing enough material for a heading to fit the rod, and using the ready-made wide hem as the bottom of the curtain. Cut and sew the heading at the top and put on a tension rod. Use matching pillow cases for the valance by opening the seams, measuring and cutting the desired length and allowing for the heading. Four pillow cases make an extra full valance. Use another tension rod for the valance, placing it higher than the shower curtain. Utilize material left for tiebacks or purchase them ready-made, securing them with stick-on hooks on the tile or wall. A shower liner on the shower rod will protect the new shower curtain when it is draped outside the bathtub.

Use additional matching pillow cases or another sheet, depending on size, for the window curtains, following the same procedure as the valance. Cover the window shade with the same material, adhering it with Elmer's glue.

When using a print, plaid, or stripe shower or window curtain, towels and carpeting should be solid colors or the same pattern as the curtains.

Add personal finishing touches: a small glass for a candle holder; an artificial flower arrangement; a saucer for a soap dish; apothecary jars for cotton balls and Q-tips holder; jars, waste baskets, and scales covered with curtain material.

MRS. JOSEPH D. (PHYLLIS) BISCOE
Kansas City, Kansas

A Bible Story Quilt

A Bible quilt which tells the Christian "Roots" story can be a real family heirloom. Patterns may be ordered from Dobbs Bargain Town, Mount Vernon, IL 62864. The cost is $1.00 per package of Old and New Testament stories. There are 13 in each package. A check for $2.50 should cover the cost of both packages and postage.

Transfers must be ironed on white material blocks, 12 inches by 13½ that are set together with solid colored strips 4½ inches wide. Length will vary according to block measures. Five blocks across and five down will make a double-size quilt.

After designs have been embroidered and set together, petal edge can be added before the quilt is put into frame. Take solid colored five-inch squares of material and fold bottom left corner up to top right. Fold top point down to bottom point. Sew rough edge to quilt top, leaving point out. Continue around the quilt until completed.

Mrs. J. B. (Jo Ann) Fustin
Danville, Illinois

Oil Finish on Refinished Furniture

To give secondhand or old furniture a carefree oil finish that lasts and stays looking nice, follow these steps:

First, strip article to be finished with "Kutzit" paint remover. Apply several coats; then give it time to loosen the old finish. A small putty knife with a blunt end is very helpful in removing stubborn finish. An SOS steelwool pad is ideal to remove last of the finish. Be sure all old finish is removed.

Second, let article dry out completely. If wood is very old or soft and absorbent, apply one very thin coat of "Minwax Antique Oil Finish" before applying stain. Let dry 24 hours. If a stain is desired, apply one coat and wipe down with paper towels. If a darker shade is desired, let dry 24 hours and apply second coat of stain, wiping down with paper towels each time.

Third, after article has dried well from stripping, apply a coat of "Minwax Antique Oil Finish" every 24 hours until the desired natural wood finish is reached. Steel-wool between coats. A cloth serves well to apply the finish.

This process gives an oil finish that is professional looking. The surface will not water-spot and is very durable under normal use. A thin coat of "Minwax Antique Oil Finish" may be applied anytime the piece of furniture begins to look dull.

MRS. BILLY G. (SUE) DUNCAN
Borger, Texas

Give Each Parsonage Your Unique Touch

It is such fun to turn a parsonage into a warm home for your family and the entertaining of God's family. It can be done with the help of a public library, a lot of dreaming, and hard work.

Visit the local garage sales twice a month with an eye for pieces that can be refinished. *Anyone* can refinish furniture. Just decide and do it.

Make napkins and tablecloths. Cut 20-inch squares for the napkins, zigzag on the machine one inch from the edge and then ravel. Use the same idea to make place mats.

Cut a round top out of plywood to fit packing barrels. Then make colorful skirts and throw pillows out of the same fabric. Patterns are available.

Make calico covers for small appliances in the kitchen and full shirred curtains to match.

For planters I collect old metal containers, paint them flat black and use them for spaces where nothing else would fit.

Baskets are fun and inexpensive. You can make wall arrangements with them, and use them for magazine holders and mail collectors.

Splash happy color all through your house. Be daring and people will think you are a seasoned decorator.

MRS. GERALD (PAULETTE) WOODS
Clovis, New Mexico

Antiquing

My addiction started innocently enough when we bought an old house with much of the contents from several generations still in it. Since that time, I have found many interesting items at auctions, house sales, garage sales, and in simply talking to people.

To decorate effectively, you can choose an item for a focal point and build around it. Some of the things we have found and use are: a player grand piano which we refinished and have in our living room (purchased at a house auction), a cherry corner cupboard from an acquaintance who wanted new shelves to display trophies; a brass bed which had to be polished, and a cut glass vase from a lawyer's estate sale. I also collect pewter and brass, which make fine accent pieces. Do not overlook the possibilities of polishing or repair when you see an article that does not look so good.

I have met many interesting people, made contacts for our church, learned many helpful facts, and have not spent nearly as much money as I would have purchasing new things at the store.

This is a hobby that has proved to be an investment because nearly all of the things have increased in value many times over what we paid for them.

> Mrs. R. Dale (Betty) Fruehling
> *Bucyrus, Ohio*

Picture Grouping

Have a wall and don't know what to do with it? Place a picture of Christ in center of area. Around this place pictures of children and/or grandchildren, and any other family members desired. This will make an attractive display, and will serve as a mute testimony to guests coming in the home that your family is built around Christ, and your activities centered in Him.

> Mrs. Harold M. (Martha) Liner
> *Camden, South Carolina*

Bathroom Accessories

Rescue small mirrors from old hand mirrors, compacts, etc. Make frames of various shapes from cardboard boxes. Frames may be covered with burlap, checked or plaid gingham, or other lightweight fabric, or they may be spray painted and trimmed with braid, ribbon, sequins, etc. Makes an inexpensive, eye-catching display.

Add elegance to solid color bathrooms linens by trimming towels and wash cloths with machine-washable ribbon, rickrack, braid, fringe, bias-cut fabric insets, or interesting appliques.

Hang an ordinary rope ladder (available in marine supply stores) from a closet tension pole for an unusual towel bar with lots of "hanging" space.

MRS. BILL (MARIE) RAY
Borger, Texas

Hanging Tips

The wall arrangements in a room can really make the difference. The important thing to remember when hanging pictures or anything on a wall is to hang them at the right level; eye level is usually correct. Before placing your arrangement of pictures on the wall determine the exact placement by arranging them first on the floor. To add variety to a wall arrangement, use other things such as mirrors, small shelves, baskets, or other decorative items. Almost anything can be hung on a wall. Use your wall arrangement to pick up the colors in your room, but try not to add any new colors. Usually hang pictures with a table, chair, or some other piece of furniture under it.

MRS. CURTIS (DONNA) MARTIN
Greensburg, Kentucky

10 Decorating Rules

Many parsonages (each one a challenge) and two years of study have been great teachers. Some valuable lessons learned which can apply to any budget are:

1. *Have one focal point.* A fireplace is a natural; some architectural feature; quite often one you create.

2. *Create space.* Let the rooms breathe even if you must remove some furniture. Save it or sell it. We all need space. It is calming.

3. *Remove clutter.* Even eclectic rooms have a sense of order. Collections look best when displayed in one place, not scattered about.

4. *Try something new.* For example, reverse the usual painting of a room: apricot ceiling, vanilla walls, mocha and blue accents.

5. *Experiment with color.* This is the best help we have as budget-minded women.

6. *Visualize your new purchases in other settings.* Functional pieces, such as bachelor's chests, can serve in almost any room. Keep woods compatible, then, when moving, you have options in placing pieces in different rooms.

7. *Mix woods.* One painted, one antiqued, and another of some different finished wood is good for most rooms.

8. *Ask advice.* Get it from some pastor's wife whose home you admire; from the best department stores; someone who has studied interior decorating will gladly talk with you about your problem areas. Take advantage of the decorating books available at your library.

9. *Try diagraming.* For instance, an art wall for your

family room is an area where you can use a variety of things, if tastefully arranged. Mix suitably framed photos with brass basket of dried flowers (weeds are everywhere), add a candleholder with an accent colored candle. Do a diagram on paper first, using graph paper, then transfer to the wall.

10. *Have the final goal in mind.* Work towards it through the years. For most of us it is a long time coming, but so rewarding!

Mrs. Gilbert A. (Vera) Rushford
San Bernardino, California

3

Entertaining

Joyful Entertaining

The key to entertaining is being yourself and being able to enjoy your guests. You can do this only by planning ahead. Over the years, it has been our privilege to entertain people from all walks of life. Since I love to entertain, this has been a happy experience, and I have learned a few methods to make entertaining easier.

Select the menu well in advance. Have food colors that will complement each other and be tasty as well. I have found it helpful to keep 3 x 5 cards with the menu served, date, number of people, and the china, silverware, tablecloth, centerpiece listed on the card.

Usually I set the table or tables early in the day of entertaining or even the night before. I prepare as many of the items as I can the day before and concentrate on the more involved recipes the day of the event. As many candles as you can light throughout the living and dining room area add an atmosphere of coziness and elegance. In the wintertime, it is a natural to have a fire burning in the fireplace.

When your guests arrive, make them feel welcome. See that their every need is met; i.e., coffee cups filled, water goblets filled, and watch carefully for plates that are becoming empty. Have the dessert plates set out ahead of time so that the transition between clearing the table and serving the dessert is fast and efficient.

Remember, the key is to plan ahead, be organized, and be yourself.

Mrs. Cecil (Joyce) Thompson
Burns, Oregon

Dressed Up Lemons

The chef at an island resort served lemon in a unique way that I would like to share. Preparing and serving the fruit in this way has several advantages:

- The lemon is large enough to provide adequate juice.
- The juice does not spatter.
- The juice does not soil the fingers as lemon is squeezed.
- The lemon is a decorative conversation piece.

Preparation: Cut the lemon in half. Place the cut side

down in the center of an 8 inch square of nylon net (your choice of color). Gather the net together at the base of the lemon and secure it with a thread or floral wire. Fluff the loose net at the base attractively. Place several on a dish to pass to guests or serve individually.

> Mrs. Mark R. (Clarice) Moore
> *Nashville, Tennessee*

Double Duty Hospitality

Entertaining two groups in succession can make good use of your time and effort. For example, give small parties on two consecutive nights. If you are making a casserole, make a double recipe. Or entertain twice on Sunday by having one group for Sunday dinner and one group for fellowship after the evening service. An average-sized cake will serve approximately 15 to 20 people, and you would have to bake only once.

The advantage of entertaining two groups in close succession is that your housecleaning and major preparation need be done only once.

> Mrs. Charles (Wilma) Peters
> *Colorado Springs, Colorado*

Balloon Party Invitations

Children's party invitations can be fun for children to make, as well as thrifty and entertaining. Buy deflated balloons, blow them up, and write the party information on the balloon with a permanent-ink felt-tipped pen. Deflate the balloons, put them in envelopes, and mail to children you wish to invite to the party. What fun it is for the invited child to blow up the balloon and find all the party information on it.

Here's another nice entertainment idea . . .

Special Cobbler Decorations

A thrifty way to use leftover pie dough is to roll it out and, using cookie cutters, cut out pretty designs to be used as fresh fruit cobbler toppings. Where we live we have an abundance of boysenberries, raspberries, apples, peaches, and apricots. I use different designs for each type of cobbler I make for home entertaining and for church social occasions. The cutout toppings may be frozen to be used at a later time.

MRS. RICK (VONNIE) SAVAGE
Napa, California

KISS System

I have had the privilege of entertaining both national and international guests in our parsonage. I have found the best tip for entertaining strangers in small or large groups is to use the KISS system—Keep It Simple, Sister.

Here are four basic suggestions:

1. *Serve with simplicity.* Serve basic foods which most people can eat and enjoy. The color of the food you choose will enhance your table and make the food more appealing.

2. *Treat your guests with a genuine warmth.* Jesus said, "If you give a cup of cold water in My name, you are doing it as unto Me." Think how you would treat Jesus if He were your guest.

3. *"Can I do something to help?"* is a frequent question asked. By all means, allow your guest to feel useful. This helps to create a friendly atmosphere.

4. *Spiritual food is important also.* We began to share the Bread of Life, God's promises, in our first pastorate. Upon completion of the meal, each person takes a promise from the promise box. If the poem on the back of the card has been set to music, the person must sing it. This has heightened the interest and often the promise has been perfectly timed for the inner needs represented.

Mrs. Jay W. (Ruth) Patton
Skowhegan, Maine

Sunday Night Buffet

Laymen love to come to the parsonage, but how can we ever have all of them? You can entertain a fairly large group at a buffet supper after church as easily as you can entertain four or six. Have them in by Sunday school class after evening church. This also helps Sunday night attendance.

For the older classes, fix chicken spaghetti—it is easy to digest. Boil chicken and debone, boil spaghetti in chicken broth. When tender, add pimento, chunks of cheddar cheese, mushroom soup, chicken, and serve with a green salad.

For other classes, serve regular spaghetti with garlic bread and salad. Spaghetti is an inexpensive dish.

If you want a change, make sandwiches. Buy day-old bread—it makes better sandwiches and is cheaper. Prepare a tasty spread by grating a two pound box of cheese; add pimento and mayonnaise and whip with an electric mixer.

Another inexpensive sandwich filling is made from boiled fryers, deboned, and chopped. When added to mayonnaise, celery, and favorite seasoning you have an excellent chicken salad. Both of these recipes make quantities of sandwiches.

Your laymen will love you for having them.

MRS. W. M. (BETTY) LYNCH
Richardson, Texas

Monthly Anniversary Reception

One way to honor the church family throughout the year is to give a monthly reception, usually the last Sunday of the month, for those having wedding anniversaries in that month, and for single adults who have had birthday anniversaries that month. All who come feel "special" for the honor bestowed upon them. What a good time to get better acquainted with people and to pray God's special blessings on them.

In the city, having this after church on Sunday evening proved effective. However, in a rural ministry, we find that the Sunday afternoon time is better for ranchers.

MRS. HARLAN (RUBY) HEAP
Ainsworth, Nebraska

Swap Luncheon

Have a recipe swap luncheon. Salads are easy to do. Each guest is asked to bring her favorite salad along with its recipe. The home where the luncheon is held provides the drink, bread, and dessert.

People love to get involved and it makes them feel needed when they bring something. Invite as many ladies as you have room to serve comfortably. This is an ideal way for the pastor's wife to get acquainted with all the ladies in the church.

> Mrs. Gerald (Paulette) Woods
> *Clovis, New Mexico*

Appetizers Make Entertaining Easier

Entertaining in the parsonage may be easier if you begin with a tray of appetizers. A tray of appetizers, hors d'oeuvres, or canapes can keep hungry guests happy and occupied while you put finishing touches on the dinner. It also answers that question, "What can I do to help?" Let one of your guests serve them.

Keep appetizers simple. A tray of vegetable pieces served with a creamy dip is a good summer dish. A small and manageable appetizer might be cherry tomatoes that have been cut in half, insides scooped out and shells drained. The tomatoes may then be filled with a chicken, tuna, or ham mixture and garnished with a wedge of olive.

On occasion I have served a fruit punch, hot spiced

tea, or tomato juice. These make extra simple appetizers with relatively little preparation.

Another idea is to cut refrigerated biscuits into four pieces. Wrap each piece of dough around an olive, roll in Parmesan cheese, and bake at 350° for 8-10 minutes.

Entertaining can be made less traumatic and more fun with the help of appetizers.

Mrs. David (Cheryl) Roland
Sherman, Texas

Entertaining Special Speakers

Our guest is going to be with us for one reason—to minister to and to spiritually serve the church. Therefore I, as hostess, need to make our guest feel at home as much as possible and to keep the atmosphere free from tensions.

In preparing for the guest, I begin early by doing extra cleaning such as washing curtains and cleaning fingerprints from walls. I want my house in tip-top shape when our company arrives. If guests come into a clean house, they are at ease, knowing that their coming has been anticipated and preparations have been made.

The day the guest arrives, I give the room where he will be staying a final cleaning. I put fresh sheets on the bed, make room in the closet for his clothing, and generally make the room as pleasant as possible. During the guest's stay, I make my washer and dryer available to him. I also keep special towels for my guests, and change them several times during the week.

Both my husband and I enjoy having company. We look forward to the fellowship that we will have. So we both relax, knowing that the house is clean and prepared for the guest. Then during his or her stay, I do a minimum of cleaning, doing only those things that are necessary. A relaxed atmosphere is important to the guest and his ability to minister at his best.

Concerning meal preparations, I am not a gourmet cook, and I do not pretend to be one, so I usually prepare simple, but hearty meals.

We have five children, so having guests has always meant that somone has had to be shifted from his bedroom. Our children have not complained about the inconvenience, because they, too, look forward to meeting someone new. We have met many of our guests as strangers and we have parted as special friends.

Mrs. Richard E. (Evelyn) Vandervort
Orbisonia, Pennsylvania

Children Help Serve Dinner

The children are excited when they know guests are coming for dinner. Each child helps in setting the table—choosing or making the centerpiece, or a little favor for each guest.

We enjoy eating at an uncluttered table and prefer the food to be served at the dining room table from the kitchen. The children rotate this special privilege of serving and look forward to their time. We all work together at getting the meal. A list of each item on the menu is made and in what dish and in what order it is to be served.

The server's plate is left in the kitchen and all are seated at the table including the server for the blessing. The server excuses himself and brings the first dish to the host who passes the food. When all are served the server returns the dish to the kitchen and brings another dish. When he has finished waiting on the table he fills his own plate in the kitchen and comes to the table to eat with the family and guests. He also has the responsibility of watching to see if all glasses and coffee cups are filled.

When all have finished eating, he takes the empty plates back to the kitchen before serving the dessert.

What an enjoying way to entertain general superintendents, district superintendents, missionaries, and evangelists. It is so relaxing for Mother and Dad, plus the children are excited about having a part in entertaining.

Mrs. E. Keith (Joan) Bottles
Danville, Illinois

Songs for Mother-Daughter Banquet

Hello, Mothers and Daughters

(Tune: "Hello, Dolly")

Hello, mothers, and hello, daughters;
It's so nice to have you dollies here tonight!
We'll celebrate, dollies; it's really great, dollies;
All the mothers and their daughters make a lovely sight.
We feel that this banquet is a bang-up banquet;
It's a sentimental, happy time for us
So . . .
We're here in style, dollies,
Give us a great big smile, dollies.
Mothers, it's nice to be with you;
Daughters, it's fine to be with you;
Dollies, it's swell to be with you tonight!

Hail, Hail, the Girls Are Here

(Tune: "Hail, Hail, the Gang's All Here")

Hail, hail, the girls are here.
What a lovely sight we are;
What a lovely sight we are.
Hail, hail, the girls are here.
So much fun without the boys!

Hail, hail, the girls are here.
Our banquet is a huge success;
Our banquet is a huge success.
Hail, hail, the girls are here.
At our Mother-Daughter fest tonight!

Doxology

Thank God for blessings from above.
Thank Him tonight for Mother's love.
Thank Him for Daughter, good and true;
Let's thank Him by the things we do.

> MRS. DWIGHT DAVID (TWILA) UMBEL
> *Ridgeville, Indiana*

Christmas with Your Church Families

This is a simple Christmas idea we used in one of our churches. We made Christmas candles for each family in the church, then made our appointed rounds to visit in each home just before Christmas. We presented each family with a candle and this message: "May the light and fragrance of the Christmas candle remind you that your pastor's family loves and cares about you." They seemed to appreciate this gesture and it did not cost us much, only our time.

MRS. MILTON (BETTY) HOOSE
Hastings, Michigan

Mother-Son Breakfast

Time: Mother's Day Sunday at 7:30 a.m.

Menu: Fresh fruits: Cantaloupe and oranges cut in fourths with rind, whole strawberries and fresh pineapple cut in chunks and served with sour cream and brown sugar.

Breads: An assortment of sweet breads, rolls, and coffee cakes.

Drinks: Orange juice, milk, coffee, and hot tea.

Decorations: Tables were decorated with live geranium plants in pots with red-and-white plaid ribbon. Plants were sold after breakfast.

Program: Special "Mother of the Year" was chosen by church board.

Tributes given by sons.

Duets by mother and son.

Panel of children answering M.C.'s questions.

Speaker is optional.

Mothers told funny incidents about their sons.

Bulletin board was decorated with pictures of mothers and sons.

MRS. BOB (GENEVA) FETTERS
Chandler, Arizona

Ladies' Day Out

The "Ladies' Day Out" fellowship is scheduled every other month at the parsonage or in a restaurant. The purpose of this activity is:

> Fellowship for the ladies within the church
> Outreach for the ladies who are not yet a part of the church
> Inspiration through devotional thoughts, often from a guest speaker

A suggested menu plan for Ladies' Day Out is:

Month 1.	Salad luncheon at the parsonage
Month 3.	Casserole luncheon at the parsonage
Month 5.	Lunch at a restaurant
Month 7.	Soup and sandwich luncheon at the parsonage
Month 9.	Dessert luncheon at the parsonage
Month 11.	Brunch at a restaurant

Food is provided potluck according to the menu plan for that month. "Ladies' Day Out" Hospitality Committee for that month provides:

> beverage
> rolls, if appropriate
> setup of tables
> cleanup

Particular problems that need to be considered with a Ladies' Day Out program are:

1. Keeping the cost as low as possible. That is why restaurant fellowship is only two times during the year.

2. Providing baby-sitting if Saturday, when most

fathers are available, is not chosen as the meeting day. However, single mothers and wives whose husbands work on Saturday will usually need an available baby-sitting service.

3. Providing "greeters" to make sure new ladies are included in the conversation.

4. Keeping the meeting as unstructured as possible. The only planned activity needs to be the meal and the devotional.

> Mrs. Michael W. (Judi) Grimshaw
> *Spokane, Washington*

4

Shower Ideas

"I Predict..."

Duplicate the following prediction sheet and give to each guest at a baby shower. Ask each guest to write her predictions about the baby-to-be, and give the papers to the expectant mother. After the baby is born, a small prize can be awarded the one who guessed most accurately.

MRS. HOMER L. (ROSAMOND) MAX
Burlington, Iowa

I PREDICT

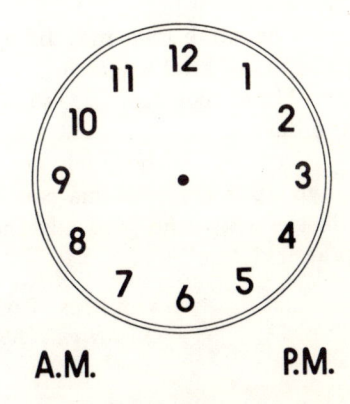

IT'S A BOY

IT'S A GIRL

A.M.   P.M.

1979

NAME

WEIGHT

LENGTH

Practical Corsages

A unique corsage for the honored lady at a baby shower may be put together from small baby things such as rattles, diaper pins, teething ring, plastic keys, using floral wire and tape. Add netting and ribbon and present it to the mother-to-be.

The same idea may be adapted for a bridal shower, using small kitchen gadgets.

These "corsages" are so practical—use your creativity and have fun!

In Hawaii where leis are given on special occasions, small appropriate items can be wrapped individually in plastic wrap and tied together with ribbon to make a practical "lei."

MRS. ROBERT C. (RUTH) KILLEN
Hilo, Hawaii

Popcorn Cake Centerpiece

This centerpiece may be used for many occasions such as birthdays, showers, parties, and holidays. It is a unique conversational piece, fun to make, and delicious to eat. Make it as follows:

- 6 qts. popped corn
- ¼ lb. oleo
- ½ cup cooking oil
- 1 pkg. (1 lb.) marshmallows
- 1 pkg. (1 lb. 6 oz.) small gumdrops
- 1 cup mixed nuts

Start marshmallows, oil, and butter in a double boiler (this takes a little time), stirring occasionally to push the marshmallows down. In your largest container, combine the popped popcorn, gumdrops, and nuts, reserving a few gumdrops for decorating. Add marshmallow mixture and mix well. Pour into buttered angel food cake pan by spoonfuls, pressing with each spoonful so you don't have an airhole in your cake. Carefully push the cake out of pan and check to see that there are colored gumdrops on the outside of the cake for color. Then add reserved gumdrops where needed. Replace the cake in pan and set in refrigerator for one hour or more to firm up. Decorate with more gumdrops if desired.

Place on a large cake plate and put a large candle in the center. Surround the cake with decorations appropriate for the occasion, such as holly, valentines, etc.

Cut wedges for serving.

MRS. GORDON G. (SHIRLEY) BELZER
Washougal, Washington

Decorated Candles

To give the honored guest at your next party or shower something very special with which to remember the event, prepare this decorated candle.

First take one of the colorful serviettes (table napkins) that you are using and cut out the design, or as much of it as you wish to use.

Next spread glue that will stick to wax on a candle that is at least two inches in diameter and five inches tall. You may wish to use a spray lacquer that is available from a hobby shop (be careful, for the lacquer is flammable).

Wrap the paper design around the candle and spray with several more coats of lacquer. Allow the candle to dry thoroughly between each coat. The paper serviette will blend right into the candle, so the edges will not be seen. Glitter may be sprinkled on the candle after the last application of glue or lacquer has been applied.

Larger candles in white and decorated with the reception serviette or table napkin make lovely wedding remembrances. Other holiday candles can be made using appropriate cut paper designs.

Mrs. William F. (Mae) Bahan
Moncton, New Brunswick, Canada

Bridal Shower Fun

What Kind of Cake?
1. The laziest cake (loaf)
2. The cake that is divine (angel food)
3. The cake that is topsy-turvy (upside down cake)
4. A kitchen utensil cake (pancake)
5. The meanest cake (devil's food)
6. The cake that isn't long (shortcake)
7. The aristocratic cake (Lady Baltimore)
8. The cake that is eaten on toast (jam)
9. Cake that lives in water (sponge)

What I Ate! (Each answer contains the word "ate.")
1. A dish (plate)
2. Opening in a fence (gate)
3. A girl's name (Kate)
4. Not on time (late)
5. To talk (prate)
6. On a calendar (date)
7. Part of a stove (grate)
8. A head (pate)
9. Part of our country (state)

10. A man's name (Nate)
11. Winter sport (skate)
12. To lie (prevaricate)
13. Evil feeling (hate)
14. We cannot escape this (fate)
15. A partner (mate)
16. Formerly used at school (slate)

>Mrs. Dwight David (Twila) Umbel
>*Ridgeville, Indiana*

Mother's Frozen Food Shower

A unique substitute for the traditional baby shower is called a "frozen food shower," and is planned by friends of the expectant mother as a social to both honor and help out. The idea is to prepare enough frozen dishes to feed the new mother's family during her first week home from the hospital.

Each friend brings her favorite recipe, such as a casserole, bread, or dessert in a disposable freezer package. The dish is completely cooked, wrapped, and sealed, ready for the freezer. On the outside of each entree are heating instructions, the name of the donor, and perhaps a copy of the recipe or ingredients.

The frozen food shower fulfills two of the greatest needs of a mother during the first weeks home from the hospital—the need for proper nutrition and the need for rest. The extra dishes packed in the freezer are a boost to the new mother's morale.

>Mrs. Ford (Barbara) Boone
>*Baton Rouge, Louisiana*

Pacifier Mints

Make Pacifier Mints for a baby shower. Start with the wafer-thin, round, colored patty mints about two inches in diameter. Put a small amount of icing in the center of each side of the mint. This icing will act as glue. On one side place a jelly bean on the icing as the nipple of the pacifier, and on the other side place a lifesaver on the icing as the handle.

These are cute and make a nice change from just regular dinner mints to go with nuts, cake, and punch for a baby shower.

MRS. CLINTON MARK (JAN) STETSON
Silverton, Oregon

No. 2 Baby Shower

In the case of a second child when you would like to do something in the way of a small shower, here is a useful idea. Arrange a manzanita or other tree branch in a pot and hold in place with plaster of paris. Decorate the branch with baby rattles and other baby items. Make little booties out of felt and ribbon and hang them on the tree for people to put money into.

MRS. JOHN (JADENE) PAYTON
Fresno, California

Bride and Groom Shower

If you need to add spice to your showers, here is an idea for the bride and groom. Honor the *couple!* The man, being a very vital part of the marriage, enjoys the festivities of the event. Invite husbands to bring gifts for the man. This will increase the size of the shower, probably more than double since some couples will come where the wife normally would not have come alone. By inviting both men and women, the honored couple will feel acceptance from the group in establishing their home and becoming "Mr. & Mrs."

One quick-moving game or icebreaker may be needed, after which the gifts and refreshments will provide the remainder of the entertainment.

MRS. JOHN R. (GLINDA) WILLIAMSON
New Albany, Indiana

Baby Shower Centerpiece

For that late summer baby shower, this melon dessert makes excellent refreshment in place of the traditional cake. Choose a well-shaped watermelon—one whose outside has not been damaged. Cut the melon lengthwise about ¾ of the way through and then half way through vertically. (See diagram.) Remove the smaller section and you already have the shape of a cradle. Use a melon baller and ball the watermelon, three cantaloupes and a honeydew melon. Mix these melon balls with fresh strawberries, white seedless grapes, green and/or maraschino cherries. Pour a small can of frozen concentrated lemonade over this mixture of fruit and refill the "cradle" with this colorful mixture. You may decorate the edges of the watermelon with gathered lace and/or ribbon pinned to the rind with ½" straight pins. It makes a lovely centerpiece as well as a tasty and unique refreshment.

> MRS. RICHARD (PHILLIS) DICKINSON
> *Paulding, Ohio*

5

Family Worship

Weekly Family Scripture

We have tried many different devotional ideas with our family. As we look back across the years, it seems the most effective was selecting a special scripture for each week of the year. This list was prepared and given to each member of the family. Together we repeated the verse before prayer each day, often taking turns or allowing the children to volunteer. We used this in our Christmas card one year and had many favorable comments.

Mrs. Reeford L. (Barbara) Chaney
Richmond, Virginia

Easy Bible Memorization

Our family chooses a chapter from the Bible, such as Philippians 4, and memorizes one verse from it each day. For example, on the second day we would each recite verses 1 and 2 at dinner. On the third day, verses 1, 2, and 3, and so on until we could recite the whole chapter. The repetition of reciting the verses daily impresses it firmly on everyone's mind. It was very rewarding to hear our 10-year-old son recite the whole fourth chapter of Philippians.

There is a "fattening" reward, such as a hot fudge sundae for each family member when we finish a long chapter.

MRS. JOHN (JADENE) PAYTON
Fresno, California

Genesis Game

Hearing the story of the creation for the first time can be confusing to children. This Genesis game has been designed to present God's plan simply. We have found that it helps children to grasp the beauty and glory of our creation.

To make the game, divide a cardboard circle into seven equal parts. Label each section for each of the seven days of the creation. In each appropriate section, draw or glue pictures of God's work for that day. Make a hole in the center of the circle. The spinner is a cardboard arrow held in place by a paper fastener. Make a set of seven cards, numbered 1 to 7, for each player. Stack all the cards together.

To play, a child spins the arrow. Whatever section of the circle the arrow stops on, he takes from the stack the card with that number. The first player to accumulate all seven cards has won.

For a more challenging game, eliminate the word labels on the sections and merely show the picture. Draw each day's work but not in sequence. The child will have to remember what was created on each day.

Another variation is to set up the game so that the seven cards must be gathered in the proper order, beginning with card one for the first day.

> Mrs. David (Cheryl) Roland
> *Sherman, Texas*

Story Book for Devotions

The *Chronicles of Narnia,* by C. S. Lewis, are excellent to read to the whole family at dinner. They have a rich spiritual undertone, particularly *The Lion, the Witch, and the Wardrobe.*

> Mrs. John (Jadene) Payton
> *Fresno, California*

Devotional Planning by Children

In our family, our children take turns planning family devotions. We have found that they can begin about the time they learn to read. This is one sure way to keep family worship on the level of their understanding; they always have interest in what they help plan.

> Mrs. Jerry D. (Anita) Ulrich
> *Owosso, Michigan*

Developing Children's Interest in Devotions

Use a family prayer board. Children can pray specifically and get involved if they see the requests on a chalkboard.

Use the timer on the stove to time the family conversational prayer time. Each member of the family offers sentence prayers until the timer rings. Be sure to say "Amen" when the timer goes off.

Let an older child read the family devotions scripture. A smaller child can count on his fingers certain words he hears, such as God, Jesus, Christ. This involves both children. Mom better do her homework to know the answer and, of course, to pick the scripture.

Family devotions can be exciting with a small amount of preparation. At the beginning of the meal the family designates the part of the devotions that follow the number.

1. Pick a chorus
2. Pray
3. Read the Bible
4. Testify (comment on a happening of the day)
5. Accompany the singing with an instrument
6. Be quizmaster regarding the scripture read
7. Solo

Before the meal, place the corresponding number of rice or beans under the plates or place mats. This can be varied, using toothpicks of different lengths.

MRS. JAMES S. (WILMA) SHAW
Walnut Creek, California

Handmade Scrolls for Family Devotions

Following is an idea that has brought much meaningful pleasure to us as we have shared together in our time of family devotions:

Family members contribute a total of 365 brief thoughts on various subjects such as encouragement, faith, inspiration, laughter.

These thoughts are to be written or typed on 2 x 3-inch slips of paper and then formed into miniature scrolls by rolling them around a pencil. Place these scrolls in a large decorative apothecary jar and keep in a convenient place for sharing as you come together for your time of family devotions.

> MRS. JERALD R. (THELMA) LOCKE
> *Bethany, Oklahoma*

A Christmas Puppet Devotional

Use commercial hand puppets or homemade sock puppets for this at-home feature. Perhaps Mom and Dad can put on the show.

Tim: Hello, Tessie; how are you this morning?
Tessie: I'm fine! I can hardly wait for Christmas, can you?
Tim: No! I add a few things to my list every day.
Tessie: Do you really have a list?
Tim: Sure, it's right here! (Holds up a long, narrow piece of paper.) Would you like to hear it?
Tessie: O.K.
Tim: Here goes— (Make a list you feel is appropriate.)
Tessie: Boy, you are asking for an awful lot. I am happy if

I get one special gift and several small ones. Are you really asking for all that?

Tim: Why not? Christmas comes only once a year. Why not make the most of it?

Tessie: You must be kidding! I think we should consider giving as well as receiving. Have you thought about any presents you would like to give others?

Tim: Oh, I usually get a small gift for everyone in the family because everybody else does. I HAVE to give something.

Tessie: I see! You know, Tim, I think you would enjoy Christmas more if you spent time making a list of things to give others.

Tim: I . . . couldn't buy big gifts.

Tessie: It doesn't have to be big gifts to show others you care about them.

Tim: I never thought of it that way.

Tessie: Oh, yes, and be sure to give Jesus a gift. The gift that would please Him most is to tell Him that you love Him. I must get home now. See you around.

Tim: Yeah, see you soon. I'm going home and make some changes on my Christmas list.

Mrs. Alton H. (Clarice) Swift
Dalton, Massachusetts

Use Children's Reading Skills

Our children are still small—eight, six, and two years old. This year during family devotions our oldest boy is reading through a Bible story book to the two smaller children. Each day they have heard the Bible in story form from the creation to many Old Testament heroes. Before the year is over, they will have progressed through the entire Bible. Our two younger children are really impressed with the fact that big brother is sharing the Bible with them.

My husband and I also share a devotional story with them about modern-day living. Generally a short scripture verse is given for them to learn. They are encouraged to remember these verses.

Mrs. Harold (Sheila) DeMott
Montpelier, Indiana

Worship for a Hyperactive Child

Do you have a hyperactive child in your Sunday school? Then you know they almost never cease moving. He or she will fidget, roam, sniffle, hum, chew, stumble, chatter, shove, climb, run, kick, scratch, jump, and fall. He cannot fit into any group situation. The child feels alone, unloved, and misunderstood everywhere he goes. The child is essentially powerless to control his bizarre behavior patterns.

It has been my experience that such a child needs the full attention of one adult. Hopefully, every church would have at least one person who would willingly give time, understanding, patience, love, and concern to such a child.

Becoming involved with Susan has been a blessing to me. Over a year ago, after having attended our Sunday school all of her 10 years, she had become too disruptive to continue participating in Children's Church. Since then I have spent the Sunday morning worship hour with her. There have been a few times when we went to the pastor's study and prayed and talked. Once we went to the parsonage. Many times we sat near the sanctuary door. A couple of times she was in something like a stupor from tranquilizers.

She has whispered to me, briefly, her concerns. Usually at prayer time she thinks of a need. Once it was worry about a 21-year-old friend who died that week from a drug overdose. God has answered prayer. Susan and I now can and often do sit near the front of the sanctuary. Not always. I let her decide. She knows whether she is having a good day or one of those impossible ones that still happen.

Just this week Susan came with this exciting news, "I got saved at camp! Now I'm not going to steal from the candy store or swear. That's sinful."

God has used me to worship Him through the needs of one of His exceptional children.

I have been blessed.

Mrs. Lorne V. (Joyce) MacMillan
Anderson, Indiana

Your Happiest Moment?

In this busy, hectic 20th century with which we all find ourselves trying to cope, our family has come up with a little game we play at night that puts us in a relaxed and happy mood as we end the day.

When we meet in the living room each evening to read God's Word and pray, we consider this question: "What was your happiest moment today?" You'd be amazed at how serious everyone becomes as they try to remember their happy moment.

These periods bring us close together as a family and many times are the highlight of the day as we sit silently and ponder every good happening.

We have been doing this for several years and it has added much to the happiness of our home.

My children live such eventful and exciting lives that their happiest moments sometimes come as a great surprise to me when they say something like: "It was when I came home from school and smelled cookies baking in the oven."

Or, "When I turned down the covers on my bed and found you had changed the sheets."

Or, "It was this morning when I walked outside and knew it would be a sunny day."

Or, "When you smiled your approval at something I had done." The thing that surprises me is the fact that it is always something very trivial and ordinary.

My husband, a very busy pastor, enjoys my asking him the same question. Once, after much thought he said, "I think it was when you brought me a glass of iced tea while I was working overtime at my desk."

This is such a beautiful way to end the day, to empty your mind of negative thoughts and replace them with positive ones.

He made my happiest moment the other evening when he answered my question with a smile and said, "My happiest moment today is right now!"

Mrs. James (Wanda) Mathews
Dunbar, West Virginia

In the Morning

"Mommy, what are we going to do in the morning?"

Soon after Becky began talking, this little question became a part of our nightly ritual of putting her to bed and saying our prayers together. Her younger brother, Jamey, followed her example on his own. So the little question has always sparked a short time of sharing with our children besides providing them with an opportunity to set goals and have at least an idea of the following day's activities. Through the years, even baby-sitters have had to be primed and ready to answer the phrase, "Tell me 'in the morning...'"

Besides bedtime, other special times a mother can have with her children are when they leave for school and when they return. A short prayer, perhaps a scripture promise they can read at the door, and a kiss send our children to school every morning. A hug, listening ear, and a peanut butter sandwich or cookie welcome them home.

> *A house should have a mother*
>   *Waiting with a hug,*
> *No matter what a boy brings home,*
>   *A puppy or a bug.*
> *For children only loiter*
>   *When the bell rings to dismiss*
> *If no one's home to greet them*
>   *With a cookie and a kiss!*
>   —HELEN WELSHIMER

Taking time—sharing, listening, understanding, longer periods of family worship—is really the "name of the game" in building relationships with our children. The results we desire will be worth every creative effort we invest.

MRS. CLARENCE J. (SUE) KINZLER
Nampa, Idaho

A Memory Board

Use a 4 x 6 plyboard (any kind or size convenient for the room). Mark into 6 inch squares. You may use a bright colored tape to do this. Secure a hook in the top of each square—about ½ inch down. Cut poster board into 6 inch squares and punch a hole in the same position as the hook on the board. Number the poster board squares beginning with No. 1 in the upper left hand corner. On the reverse side print a portion of a scripture verse. On another numbered card print the remaining portion of the same verse—such as, Card No. 1, "In the beginning God—." Print Bible verses in this divided manner on all the numbered cards and hang them on the hooks with the numbered side showing.

Divide the children into two groups, then take turns to see which side can find the most completed scriptures by calling out card numbers and remembering where the parts of the verses are located and matching them for a completed verse.

Several sets of cards keeps them learning. Prizes are also fun to receive.

Mrs. M. Bert (Lola) Daniels
Oklahoma City, Oklahoma

Traps Are to Stay Out Of

As young boys, our two sons had great times capturing squirrels and then turning them loose again.

A box, a stick, a heavy cord, and a few kernels of corn—everything was set just so. Then they waited around the corner of the house until the precise moment to pull the cord that removed the stick, causing the box to drop on Mr. Squirrel and the corn. What shouts of victory—"We caught him, Mom. We caught him!" The fun was in catching him, turning him loose, then setting the trap for a repeat performance with another unsuspecting animal.

Satan sets traps, too; but, they are not for fun. He purposes them to be for "keeps."

Satan has eye traps ("Oh, that program isn't so bad ... Hey, look at this cheap-o magazine ... and ...).

He has ear traps ("Want to hear a good story—only promise not to tell your mother").

And tongue traps ("Just tell a little lie and get out of trouble").

He also has hand traps ("Go ahead and take it, they'll never miss it").

And feet traps ("Let's sneak into the ball game and save our money for popcorn").

Satan's traps are called temptations, and he is out to catch everyone he can. The Bible says, "A trap doesn't snap shut unless it is stepped on" (Amos 3:5, TLB). Our best safety amid Satan's traps is to stay away from them. He traps for "keeps."

MRS. FLOYD H. (CAROL) POUNDS
Peoria, Illinois

6

Living on a Shoestring Budget

Six Rules for Stretching the Budget

1. **Sales**—Buy furniture, linens, household, and camping equipment only when they are on sale. Here it pays to buy good quality and respected brands. Wait until July sales to buy summer clothing, and January sales to buy winter clothing. Shop at the good quality stores for most clothing needs, especially for items like coats and suits. Buy children's needs in a size larger for the next season. If you sew, fabric sales and remnant counters

offer additional savings. Put big hems in children's clothes and have fun adding ruffles, borders, and cuffs to make an outfit over.

2. **Grocery Advice**—Buy only food that gives good nutrition. Strike out "junk foods" such as soft drinks and chips. Eliminate pizzas, pastries, and such that give low "mileage" for your food dollar. Cultivate your family's appetite for fresh fruit and vegetables, whole wheat bread, cheese and egg dishes. Garnishes, music, flowers, and candles can transform the most frugal meal into a banquet. Make "eating out" a rare treat.

3. **Plan Car Use**—Correlate driving "hither and yon" and taxiing family around. It does no harm for youngsters to ride bicycles or walk.

4. **Handy Woman**—Learn to "do it yourself" in repairing, fixing, and redecorating. There are dozens of people who will tell you how if you ask.

5. **Save all you can**—Always spend less than you make, and regularly put some money into a savings account. Regardless of how little this may be, it will give the feeling of being able to "make it" on your income.

6. **Count your blessings**—Be thankful and grateful for what you have and especially for the privilege of serving God, our fellowmen, and the church.

MRS. WILLIAM F. (MAE) BAHAN
Moncton, New Brunswick, Canada

Vegetable Centerpiece

As a centerpiece for our kitchen table, I fill a bowl or basket with onions and potatoes which we usually keep on hand. When I have fruit that does not need refrigeration, I add this to the centerpiece. This helps me keep up with our supply of vegetables and serves when flower arrangements are not possible. When guests are coming, you may add cabbage, egg plant, or squash for variety and color.

      Mrs. Reeford L. (Barbara) Chaney
      Richmond, Virginia

Now Hear Ye This

A good way to give our tight budgets some breathing room is to adapt to our own use this New England motto:
    Eat it up!
    Wear it out!
    Make it do!
    Or do without!

      Mrs. Walter (Lola) Williams
      St. David, Illinois

Making Dresses Do Triple Duty

Recently I heard about a lady who hired her sewing done but still used ingenuity and forethought and, as a result, got her money's worth out of her dresses.

First, she always purchased better-than-the-usual-grade of fabric, choosing cloth that would wear a long time and remain attractive.

Secondly, she picked her pattern with care, mentally visualizing how it could be refashioned at least twice when she tired of the present style. A full skirt became, in time, a narrow skirt. Still later, the slimmer-skirted dress, a jumper.

Using one's imagination, one might carry this plan a step or two farther. The jumper could end up as a skirt and vest or a child's slack outfit.

>Mrs. Russell E. (Pauline) Spray
>*Lowell, Michigan*

Shoestring Shopping and Eating

Necessity is the mother of invention. When there is less money, it is simply a challenge to rise to the occasion. On the night before I buy groceries, I plan my weekly menu. One main meal per day, varying breakfasts and light lunches. I do this on a legal size pad. My menus may look something like this:

FRIDAY
Lasagna
Salad
French Bread

SATURDAY
Fish
Baked Potato
Mixed Vegetables
Salad

SUNDAY
Chicken Curry
Rice, Green Beans
Salad, Whole Wheat Rolls

MONDAY
Quiche Lorraine
Carrots
Green Salad

TUESDAY
Six-layer Tuna Salad
Whole Wheat Rolls
Strawberries & Bananas

WEDNESDAY
Hamburger Steaks
Baked Potato
Salad

THURSDAY
Fried Chicken   Broccoli
Steamed Rice   Corn Bread

GROCERIES (Based upon my menu)

3 lbs. hamburger	Swiss cheese
salad materials: lettuce tomatoes, onions, celery	carrots rice broccoli
Salad dressing	2 pkg. rolls
5 lbs. potatoes	strawberries and bananas
2 lbs. fish	
2 chickens	tuna
1 pkg. frozen mixed vegetables	olives and avocados pie shells
eggs	soaps
3 lbs. bacon	papers
bread	

I buy *only* what's on my list, and I tally up the total before checking out. You vary each week according to your needs and likes.

I take the menu and tape it to the refrigerator—in full view. You can always switch days and your family will love the idea of a menu around—just like a restaurant.

Mrs. Gerald (Paulette) Woods
Clovis, New Mexico

A Christmas Card Design

One year I cut inexpensive Christmas wrapping paper into 5" x 8" sheets. I used the church mimeograph to copy a poem on the back side of paper (it could be typed or handwritten):

We searched and searched for a present for you,
But couldn't find a thing, not one thing would do.
And then we found it; had it with us all the time.
Didn't cost much either, not even a dime.
So we wrapped it all up in paper and ribbons so gay.
Just this . . . about each of you, something nice to say!

Then we wrote in the name of each person and told what we really did appreciate about them. I folded the paper into thirds, and tied with the inexpensive curling ribbon.

>Mrs. Harold (Rachel) Ellis
>*Farnam, Nebraska*

Gourmet TV Dinners

At one church move, we discovered that my husband's salary would be lowered $60.00 per month, and I was asked not to continue teaching school. Now that was a challenge for a family of five: a total of $500 less monthly income.

The Friday fun dinners of giant tenderloins with milkshakes became a memory. On a "shoestring" budget, how can those pleasurable occasions be replaced? The aluminum trays from TV dinners was an answer. Why not prepare frozen surprise dinners from the entertaining leftovers? We always have our best food for guests, and leftovers should never be thrown away. So after a week of beans and rice, frozen special leftovers in TV dinner trays without labels provided surprises we all anticipated. These meals were hilarious, and blessed with out of the ordinary salad and dessert. No wonder our children begged for company.

>Mrs. R. J. (Maudie) Clack
>*Madison, Wisconsin*

How to Budget

1. **Never over charge.** Buy only what you can pay for at the time. Keep a charge at just one store.

2. **Look for bargains.** That goes for sales, too.

3. **Learn to sew.** It is much cheaper to sew than to buy ready-made clothes. There are many simple methods to sew now. Anyone can learn. I know, because I learned; and if I can, anyone can.

4. **Plan your meals.** I guarantee you will find it is cheaper to cook and shop that way. Learn to can garden vegetables.

5. **Don't shop with a lot of coupons.** You will buy things you really don't need. Of course use the coupons for products you need to purchase.

6. **Keep track of monthly bills in a notebook.** Then write down for each week. Learn to live on a budget. If you don't have the money, don't buy.

7. **Always tithe.** Do it cheerfully.

8. **Trust God.** Pray some things in. Remember John 16:24—"Ask, and ye shall receive, that your joy may be full."

9. **Don't be neighbor keeper-upper.** That's not in the spirit of Christ.

10. **Learn:** "In whatsoever state I am, therewith to be content" (Philippians 4:11).

Mrs. G. A. (Myrna) Hazlett
Warren, Ohio

Recipe for Hungry Teens

For an easy and inexpensive main dish that will especially satisfy hungry, teenage boys, try the following:

Saute the following in a little cooking oil:
    4 frankfurters cut into ¼ inch coin-like slices
    1 onion, chopped
    1 green pepper, cut into one inch strips.
Add to the above:
    6 cooked and diced white potatoes
Brown all together in a skillet, adding salt and pepper to taste.

Serve with a salad of your own choosing.
This makes a little meat go a L-O-N-G way!

MRS. WILLIAM W. (DORIS) RESTRICK
Wallingford, Connecticut

Double-Knit Thrift

Draperies made from colorful double-knit fabric give an informal dining area a fresh, lively look. A matching tablecloth trimmed with wide lace adds a smart touch. A matching place mat in double knit, with a plastic mat underneath, is a time saver if you have a child who is apt to make spills.

For heavier draperies, a double thickness of material can be used in place of a lining. Often this double-knit material can be found on sale for as little as $1.00 per yard. It is usually 60 inches wide and requires no ironing.

MRS. RONALD L. (JOAN) WHITTENBERGER
Uhrichsville, Ohio

A Bridal Attendant's Headpiece

For the attendants' headpieces in our daughter's wedding we purchased small flower wreath candle rings for a dime each and added ruffles of tulle. Although they cost practically nothing, these circlets were attractive and matched the bouquets of artificial and fresh flowers perfectly.

MRS. RUSSEL E. (PAULINE) SPRAY
Lowell, Michigan

Drapes and Tablecloths

Sheets can be used to make drapes, lined or unlined, and are easy to work with and save money. They can also be used, solids or prints, for round tablecloths cut to the exact size needed.

MRS. REEFORD L. (BARBARA) CHANEY
Richmond, Virginia

Budgeting

Living within our means seems to be a difficult task in our day of materialism. However, it can be done with dignity. The greatest lesson a parsonage pair can ever learn is to live within a budget and to pray in the extras. A budget takes discipline. It eliminates childish or impulsive buying. If God can trust us with a small budget, He may honor us and give added blessings. The mistake that is made by so many is to cash a paycheck and then start dishing it out. It will never work.

Don't try to keep up with other pastors on the district. If they drive a prestige car, let them worry with the payments. Do what you can where you are. Set up a budget, stay with it, give liberally.

Mrs. David J. (Sandra) Felter
Bloomington, Indiana

Inexpensive Tablecloths

Our family enjoys having meal guests. But it seems difficult to keep up with nice tablecloths, so I often purchase double knit material in the desired color. I especially like greens and blues. You can cut the fabric and leave the edge as is. You can add hemming lace on edge, or edge stitch it on the sewing machine, or crochet around the edge with a very simple stitch. It is easy to cut round cloths and add side pieces to make a 70 or 72 inch tablecloth.

Mrs. Reeford L. (Barbara) Chaney
Richmond, Virginia

Instant Stuffing

To save time and money, I keep a plastic bag in my freezer for any leftover bread items; (biscuits, cornbread/muffins, croutons, and various bits and pieces of bread). Crumble the leftovers into the sack so when it is time for stuffing a fowl or making dressing, you can take it out and use accordingly. Saves wasted bread scraps and gives an excellent flavor.

You'll also want to try . . .

Quick Vegetable Soup

I keep a gallon plastic container in my freezer into which goes all leftover vegetables and beef. So, when I want it—*presto!*—homemade vegetable soup. It is quick and, with the addition of broth from a soup bone and some tomato juice, I have soup to share with our elderly, the sick, neighbors, and us. They are always appreciative and my expense has been at a very minimum.

MRS. BILL (SHIRLEY) REED
Bicknell, Indiana

Guidelines for Shopping

Here are some of the grocery shopping guidelines that I follow:
- Find a "no nonsense" food store that does not have promotional games or contests.
- Plan menus for a week at a time, then list the items you will need. Stick to your menus and your list.
- Plan to shop just one day a week and don't allow yourself to return to the store until the next scheduled visit.
- Take the exact amount of cash to the store that you plan to spend—no checkbook. A calculator is helpful for keeping track of the totals as you shop.
- When possible, purchase "house brand" or the new generic (plain label) products.
- Go directly to the aisles where your "list" items are found rather than canvassing the entire store.
- Don't purchase any "snack foods" except popcorn that you can pop yourself.

- Don't purchase any mixes; make everything from "scratch."
- Make all bread purchases from a day-old bread store or from the "reduced" rack of the grocery store—or bake your own!
- Never use bottled milk in cooking, use only powdered.
- Check the "reduced for quick sale" cart each week.
- Make all soups yourself rather than using canned or packaged.
- Make some "meatless" meals such as omelets, bean or lentil soups, and cheese casseroles; all are good sources of protein.
- Think of meat as an *accompaniment* rather than the main course, and purchase it according to the number of servings you can get out of it.
- Limit the cleaning aids that you purchase, buy one or two aids that can be used for all the cleaning jobs.
- Don't purchase or use paper towels or paper napkins. Make cloth napkins out of a "no iron" material and use them at every meal. Be sure to make a large enough supply to last from one washday to the next.
- Compare prices on everything. I have found that liquid laundry detergent (the quarter-a-cup-per-load-type) is the most economical, as are the "single" rolls of bathroom tissue.
- Don't waste anything.
- Have a special fund for entertainment so that you can purchase food items for company—but use it only for that!
- Don't give up after a failure. It becomes easier as you form the habit of economizing.

MRS. R. JAMES (LYNN) BLEDSAW
Kenosha, Wisconsin

7

Inexpensive Gifts

Decoupage Announcements

For several years I have decoupaged graduation announcements with their pictures for our graduating high school and college seniors. The following steps indicate how to make the plaque:

1. Stain both sides of a board approximately 6 inches by 12 inches.
2. Cut around the name card and the announcement itself. Burn around the edges of these and scrape off the charred, burned paper. You want a brown edge.

3. Glue the pieces on the board with Mod Podge (available from a hobby shop), working out all air bubbles. Place the name card at the top, then the picture with the emblem from the announcement beside it, then the announcement itself.
4. Let dry overnight.
5. Very lightly stain the announcement and name card to make it look antique.
6. Apply two or three coats of Mod Podge to entire plaque. Let dry after each coat.
7. Apply one coat of Crackle-It (also a hobby shop item) on the announcement part only. Let it dry 24 hours or more to allow it to crackle.
8. Apply stain on announcement part only to fill in cracks. Wipe off excess stain.
9. Apply one coat of Protect-It or clear varnish.
10. Put decorative hanger on top.

This can also be done with wedding announcements. They make attractive keepsakes. Students and couples seem to really appreciate them.

MRS. BUD (SUE) PRENTICE
Shreveport, Louisiana

Gifts for the Church Board

Each year at Christmas, we express our personal appreciation for our local church board by presenting them with a handmade gift, usually at a Christmas dinner in our home.

The gifts have varied over the years. At times we have given homemade jellies or pumpkin bread, wrapped in

Christmas ribbon. One year we presented my Russian tea mixture in apothecary jars, along with the recipe.

Among handcrafted wooden gifts were decoupaged plaques of the praying hands. We took the pictures of the praying hands from the place mats which we were able to buy for two cents each at a local restaurant.

Ecology boxes with dried flowers, beans, split peas, and corn, were also a fun gift to make. Small deer, bees, mushrooms, or butterflies added a pleasant touch and individualized each box.

Another useful wooden item was a decorated breadboard made from oak, each with the board member's initial on the front side.

None of these gifts has been expensive to make; some have been much more time consuming than others; but all have been greatly appreciated by our board members.

Mrs. Harold (Sheila) DeMott
Montpelier, Indiana

Thank-you Gift for VBS Workers

Along with an appreciation card or note, I give workers a loaf of homemade bread, jelly, cake, or fruit breads. The workers are tired and the thought of something homemade is always nice to anticipate. If fruit is not available for jelly, a jar of apple juice, grape juice, or cherry juice, works fine. Use inexpensive glasses or coffee mugs for containers, which will also later serve as a nice remembrance.

Mrs. Don (Ann) Cannon
Santa Fe, New Mexico

Lambs for Newborns

I searched carefully and prayerfully for a meaningful new-baby gift. It had to be something special, with spiritual significance.

And then I found it. A fluffy, white stuffed lamb. Along with each lamb I include a poem or a copy of the 23rd psalm.

My gift lamb has become a cherished item that is anticipated by each new mother. It is suitable for a boy or a girl, has a spiritual significance, can be kept for years, and is reasonably priced.

Here is one of the verses I have used. Perhaps you will want to write your own.

> *Jesus loves His little lambs,*
>   *The Bible tells us so.*
> *With loving care He keeps His flock*
>   *And watches each one grow.*
>
> *May this little lamb remind you*
>   *Of the Shepherd's constant care,*
> *May you and Baby [or baby's name] always*
>   *know*
>   *He's with you everywhere.*
>
> *Since lambs follow sheep*
>   *We also pray,*
> *Guide Mommy and Daddy*
>   *Every day.*

          Mrs. Ronald L. (Joan) Whittenberger
          Uhrichsville, Ohio

Place Mats and Napkins

To easily make colorful place mats and napkins, purchase ¾ yard of any quilted material and ¾ yard of solid color blend of polyester and cotton that matches the quilted fabric. You will also need three packages of rickrack of the same color.

Cut four 13 inches by 19 inches mats of quilted material. Hem under ¼ inch all around. Sew rickrack all around on top side or underneath for tips to show. Cut four pieces of solid color for napkins, 12½ inches square. Turn under ¼ inch and sew or zigzag around with matching or contrasting thread.

To make pockets for napkins, cut four pieces 4½ by 3½, fold down across top, and sew or zigzag. Fold two sides ¼ inch and sew neatly to left side of place mat 2 inches from edge. Fold napkins to fit pocket and insert.

Scraps from the place mats can be used to make matching pot holders. Place mats can be made in different colors, using remnants or by purchasing 1/3 yard of several prints.

If these are made for your home, buy extra material to make bright cafe curtains for the kitchen.

MRS. J. B. (JO ANN) FUSTIN
Danville, Illinois

Handmade Wooden Puzzles

Wooden puzzles are great for young children. Purchase a child's coloring book with large simple pictures. Using carbon paper, trace onto one-half to three-fourths inch pine (or whatever suitable wood scraps you have). Cut out the square picture with a jigsaw. Depending on the age of the child, cut into three to five pieces with interlocking parts. Sand so there are no rough places. Either paint or use felt-tips to color the puzzle. You may want to varnish to seal the wood.

> Mrs. Orbin N. (Marsha) Crouch
> *Custer City, Oklahoma*

Baby Jar Gifts

Those empty baby food jars are very useful items for inexpensive gifts.

- Fill with hard candies and tie with a bright ribbon for a small hospital gift for children or adults
- Fill with home-canned jam or jelly
- At Christmastime, I fill these little jars with Friendship Tea, cut out a gingham square for under the lid, and tie with a matching ribbon for my ladies' group. The Friendship Tea recipe is:

>   3 cups sugar
>   2 cups orange drink mix (such as Tang)
>   1 cup instant tea (lemon flavored)
>   cinnamon, cloves, candy red-hots

Serve 2 tsp. to 1 cup boiling water (put instructions on jar).

Another thing I have enjoyed doing is to make cutout cookies for special days—Christmas, Thanksgiving, Valentine's Day, Halloween—and distribute to all our senior adults. They seem to look forward to this small treat from me. It brings back happy childhood memories.

> Mrs. Perry (Mary) Winkle
> *Lewiston, Idaho*

Emergency Purse Kit

Cut two-inch by six-inch red and green felt strips with pinking scissors. Pin the following items in an attractive arrangement onto the strips: straight pins, small gold safety pins, needles threaded with at least two different colors of thread, a larger safety pin with small buttons threaded onto it. About one inch from each end, cut a diagonal slit about one-half inch long. Thread about 8 to 12 inches of grosgrain ribbon through the back of this, then roll up with articles on the inside. Tie a bow knot with the leftover ribbon. This makes a very attractive and useful item to have in your purse.

These may be used as small gifts for each lady of the church at Christmastime. Their appreciation lasts all year.

MRS. TOMIE S. (ELLA) MARTIN
Grand Saline, Texas

Washcloth and Guest Towel Holder

This attractive washcloth and/or guest towel holder for a bathroom may be given as a gift to a friend, or as a Mother's Day project in a Sunday school class, or as a vacation Bible school craft project.

The following materials are needed:
- ¼ yard of white burlap
- 2 yards of ¼-inch ribbon of desired color
- Two ¾-inch round wooden beads
- ¼-inch diameter wood dowel, 4 inches long

6-inch diameter wooden ring
4-inch diameter wooden ring
Glue (Elmer's or craft)
Scissors

Step 1: Cut a strip of burlap 28 inches in length and 4 inches wide. If burlap is wrinkled, press with warm iron.

Step 2: Cut two pices of ribbon, each 24 inches long. Glue to outside edges of burlap. Glue a piece of ribbon (4 inches) down top middle of burlap. (See diagram.)

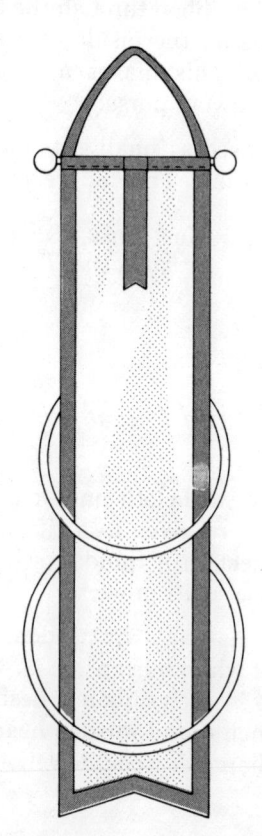

92

Step 3: Cut bottom edge of burlap into an inverted V. Glue strip of ribbon around edge of V.

Step 4: Measure 6 inches up from bottom of burlap and place the 6-inch wooden ring. Make a 2-inch fold down over top of ring with burlap. Staple and glue.

Step 5: Measure 3 inches up from top of large wooden ring and place the 4-inch ring. Proceed as in Step 4.

Step 6: Attach the 4-inch wooden dowel rod to top of burlap strip. Roll burlap around rod once. Glue in place, allow to dry.

Step 7: Glue 8-inch piece of ribbon to outside edge of dowel rod.

Step 8: Add one wooden bead to each end of dowel rod.

Step 9: Set aside and allow to dry for about one-half hour. After drying, insert your favorite washcloth and/or guest towel in each ring and hang in your guest bathroom.

MRS. CHUCK (ANNA MARIE) LOCKARD, JR.
Germantown, Ohio

Memory Box

Gifts with a personal touch have a sentimental value and mean a great deal to the recipient. In our church one of the most cherished gifts is the memory box which I make. This unique gift is made from a wooden ecology box which you can make or purchase in a craft shop. The box is filled with memorabilia and meaningful miniatures. Suggested items to be included are photographs, tiny dried flowers, pieces of bark and fabric, craft store miniatures, and spiritual symbols.

A memory box for a bride and groom might contain the following:

- The couple's favorite scripture verses written on tiny handmade scrolls with a small cross or dove in the foreground.
- A photo of the church with dried flowers and plastic tiny trees around it.
- A photo of the bride's home with a tiny cutout photo of the bride as a child set in front to give a 3-D effect. The same can be done for the groom.
- Parents' photographs, cut out and arranged to give a 3-D effect. Surround with tiny plastic greens or make a background of pretty fabric.
- Other squares can be filled with tiny dried flower arrangements or something colorful.

After all square pigeonholes are filled and the effect is pleasing, glue the glass cover, which usually comes with the ecology box, in place. Fine gold braid may be glued around the edge of the glass to give a special touch. A keytype hanger should be screwed into place on top of the box.

Memory boxes are popular gifts for weddings, anniversaries, farewells. At Christmas they make good gifts for Sunday school teachers.

MRS. RONALD L. (JOAN) WHITTENBERGER
Uhrichsville, Ohio

The Gift Shelf

The most inexpensive gift idea in the world is my "gift shelf." I got the idea from my mother's inexhaustible "gift box" upstairs at home.

The best time to start one is early in marriage when the initial gift avalanche comes—you can plainly see that one ice bowl and two ice buckets will be more than adequate for your needs. So at least one of the ice buckets goes into the gift box. And though you treasure the Betty Crocker cookbook you received, you surely cannot use two identical books—so into the gift box one goes.

Farther along in married life, in times of short funds or busy days, the gift shelf or box brings forth many selections of duplicates or unreturnables received as Christmas or birthday gifts. You may even find a lovely flowered sheet or decorator item that you bought on sale.

This is not to say you do not treasure the gifts and those who gave them; you do. This idea is only to use those duplicates or unreturnables because of wrong size or color, wrong store or state, or unsuitables you simply cannot use.

One last suggestion: pin or tape a small paper to the gift stating from whom you received it, so you are reminded to wait until the *next* pastorate to share it with another.

NAME WITHHELD

Christmas Ornament Gifts

Christmas ornaments make an ideal gift for many occasions. The price range is great, so they fit any budget. Not only can they be given to special friends and relatives at Christmas, but they make unique wedding and baby gifts. A complete set can be purchased at a reasonable price by purchasing precut kits which include paint and all the items needed to finish them. The sets can be completed long before the special occasion.

MRS. KENNETH W. (CAROLYN) WADE
Fort Wayne, Indiana

A Gift of Inspiring Scripture

I take the name of the person for whom a gift is intended and do an acrostic with each letter of her name, using God's precious promises. For *WILCON* I submit this example:

With God all things are possible (Mark 10:27).
I will never leave thee, nor forsake thee (Heb. 13:5).
Lo, I am with you alway, even unto the end of the world (Matt. 28:20).
Come unto me . . . and I will give you rest (Matt. 11:28).
Obey my voice, and I will be your God (Jer. 7:23).
None of them that trust in him shall be desolate (Ps. 34:22).

It can be kept simple or go more elaborate. You may wish to letter or type the gift on a 3 x 5 card, slipped into a greeting card, or framed or decoupaged.

Mrs. J. Richard (Virginia) Lord
Moultrie, Georgia

Green Plant and Strawberry Box

I have found plants to be inexpensive gifts that are easily attainable, especially if you grow your own.

A strawberry begonia potted in a small square container can become a beautiful spring centerpiece.

Place it inside an old-fashioned wood strawberry crate. Fill in the empty space between the pot and crate with excelsior. This gives the appearance of straw. Add artificial strawberries and blooms which can be purchased from most dime stores. Make a red gingham bow and place near the center of the pot. The centerpiece gives the appearance of a real strawberry plant in full bloom and bearing fruit. Visitors will take a closer look.

Mrs. James L. (Joan) Stewart
Memphis, Tennessee

8

Unique Outreach

⸙

City Hall Bible Studies

"A door was opened unto me of the Lord." I refer specifically to a weekly Bible study held in the Cambridge City Hall, Cambridge, Mass. The Catholic city manager who attended one of these Bible studies commented, "Cambridge needs this!" Mary D., an atheist, found Christ as her personal Savior in City Hall. Today Mary is a faithful member of our Cambridge Church of the Nazarene and is active in our Nursery Department.

Tom S., an accountant in the Model Cities Department of Cambridge, attended the Bible studies regularly. He felt a call to the ministry and enrolled for ministerial studies at Eastern Nazarene College. Tom graduated this spring. After seminary, he plans to enter the full-time ministry.

Dora H., a young hospital worker, came to the Bible studies and soon felt a hunger to know Christ personally. She invited me to her home for more Bible study. I soon learned that Jehovah's Witnesses were calling on Dora and conducting their own weekly study group in her home. I was asked to encounter them. Dora and her husband chose to follow Christ. Today they are attending our Cambridge church with their two sons and hope to join the church soon.

Bible studies in City Hall and in homes are my first love! For many years I have found this type of outreach most joyful and rewarding. A large percentage of the converts have joined the church and have become good workers. Another good feature of this ministry is that as an active minister's wife, one can schedule 1 or 10 studies per week as time and circumstances permit. Pray to get started, pray to continue, and God will bless with fruitful results.

Mrs. Robert F. (Wilma) Utter
Cambridge, Massachusetts

Pastry Evangelism

Cake decorating may be used as a unique method of outreach. I bake, decorate, and personally deliver birthday and anniversary cakes to each adult in the church. This is especially beneficial in establishing friendship with unsaved husbands or wives of the church family. Older people are the most grateful because their birthdays are often ignored or forgotten. They are thrilled with this remembrance from the parsonage family.

> MRS. PAUL (RAMONA) CONE
> *Fullerton, California*

Stop and Go Appreciation

One of the nicest ways to show appreciation for a vacation or trip-bound friend, baby-sitter, or prospective family is to make a "Stop and Go" box.

Decorate a good sturdy box (shoe or gift boxes are ideal) with pretty paper. Use solid, bright paper with the words "Stop and Go" cut from magazines or cut from colorful construction paper. Scatter the words "Stop" and "Go" all over the box. Wrap the lid separately from the box, so that it can be easily removed.

Fill the box with some of your favorite munching "goodies." Maybe you would like to involve your own family by baking your favorite cookie or candy recipe. Involving the family will teach the children to show love and concern for others. It will also provide them with something to do on those "bored" days.

Goodies may be baked ahead of time and frozen; the boxes may be decorated on those cold winter evenings and stored until needed.

Enclose a short note with the treats, wishing the family a good time and safe return. A favorite scripture may also be included.

> MRS. JAMES R. (CHRIS) BLANKENSHIP
> *St. Marys, Ohio*

Post Office Thank-you

With so much mail coming into and going out of the church office and parsonage, the post office staff may, at times, feel overworked. On every Friday the 13th, try baking a cake for the crew at the post office to show your appreciation for their service. Friday the 13th occurs only a few times during the year, so this does not become a chore.

Take along packages of small paper plates and plastic forks so there is no fuss or bother for anyone. This will create goodwill, and you might even get a smile when you take in that big stack of newsletters.

> Mrs. Don (Coralyn) Davis
> *Charleston, South Carolina*

A Friendship or Prayer Partner Tea

Ask ladies to bring a teacup to a designated area a week or so before the tea in an unwrapped box with their names enclosed.

After all have arrived at the tea, give the following explanation:

1. Ladies will find their names by their teacups, but the cup will be on a different saucer.
2. Remain seated until every lady finds her teacup.
3. Following prayer, each one locates the lady who has the saucer for her cup. That lady should have the cup for her saucer.
4. These two ladies will exchange cups and then go to be served.
5. After being served, partners will sit at any of the

tables to get acquainted with each other and with those seated at that table.

The following forms may be handed out or may be at the tables. These are to be filled out and exchanged by partners. The ladies build up a friendship or become prayer partners for the year.

```
Name: _____
Address: _____
City: _____ Zip _____
Phone: _____
Husband's Name: _____
Children: _____
           _____

Secular Work: _____
Husband's Work: _____
Anniversary: _____
Birthday: _____
```

Mrs. Irving (Eleanor) Sullivan
Bakersfield, California

Lunch Box Fellowship

On the last Sunday of each month, pass around two metal lunch boxes. Each person or family who wishes to participate writes his name on a slip of paper and drops it in the box. The boxes are shaken and then passed around again. Each one who puts in a name draws one out. If he draws his own name, he puts it back and takes another.

The idea is to entertain the family whose name you draw in some way during the following month. You can have them for a snack after church, or invite them for a meal anytime during the month, or take them out for a Coke or a full meal.

Do not take the same name twice. During the year you will have fellowship with 24 different families—you entertain 12, and 12 entertain you. Be sure to have each family notify the one whose name they drew the same evening as the drawing.

The church family really get to know each other this way. It is especially nice for the pastor's family, for you can entertain individual families without criticism.

Mrs. Cloyce C. (Elaine) Cunningham
Ritzville, Washington

Cradle Roll Outreach

Outreach through the Cradle Roll is an effective way to discover new families. Feelings of pride and great joy are evident when a new baby joins the family circle.

Ceramic booties are comparatively inexpensive to make and give. These can be purchased in greenware, painted and decorated, and then fired. Or they can be purchased as cold ceramics that have already been fired; you then paint and decorate them.

An attractive brochure should be prepared containing congratulations to the family of the new baby, the days and times of the regular services of the church, and an invitation to visit these services.

In most areas, birth announcements are printed in the local newspaper. A few days after the birth announcement has appeared in the newspaper, a personable lady from the church should call on the new mother with the gift of *one* bootie containing a small plant and the prepared brochure.

in pairs. So the new mother is told that when she brings the new baby to church, she will receive the mate to the first bootie.

Do not forget to request the privilege of placing the baby on the Cradle Roll.

MRS. WILLIAM (GLADYS) HURT
Lowell, Michigan

A Ladies' Slumber Party

Who: All ladies ages 18-108
Where: Parsonage
Time: 7:30 p.m. to 9 a.m.
Bring: Sleeping bag, night clothes, and snack foods
Purpose: 1. To get to know one another better
           2. To have a spiritual lift

The senior citizens seem to enjoy this activity the most. Many ladies have never been to a slumber party, "so they can make up for lost time."

In the early evening have get-acquainted activities and end with a devotional time about 11:30. Those who wish to may visit while others may go on to bed.

Serve a continental breakfast about 8 a.m., with devotions following.

MRS. HERBERT (CAROLYN) IRELAND
Port Orchard, Washington

Bible Clubs

Get ladies in your church neighborhood to have one-hour children's Bible clubs for you. All they have to do is invite the children and greet them as they arrive. Children's workers from the Sunday school will be the teachers. The club should meet once a week for 6 to 10 weeks. Announce anything exciting going on at your church in the children's department. You might even plan some events, so they can be announced. Let the lady of the home invite the children's mothers to slip in and watch the children at club once in a while.

This will introduce your church to people and open doors in an exciting new way.

MRS. ALLEN H. (VIRGINIA) DACE
Denver, Colorado

Outreach by the Loaf

A suburban church tried this novel way of welcoming every new member that moved into their town: Each lady of the church baked six small loaves of bread (banana, date and nut, cranberry, lemon, etc.) in 2" x 5" foil pans. Each loaf was wrapped neatly in foil and labeled. All the loaves were stored in one freezer to be used by the visitation committee.

When calling on a newcomer to town, the visitor took a loaf of bread with an appropriate greeting attached, along with the usual local church brochure and a copy of the special *Herald of Holiness*.

The name, address, and phone number of the baker could be attached as one person the family can call if they need help in some way.

This idea may be made into a group project for teens as well as ladies.

MRS. WILLIAM W. (DORIS) RESTRICK
Wallingford, Connecticut

Love Breakfast

About three weeks before Valentine's Day, I was awakened about midnight with a God-given idea. He told me to show the ladies of our church how much I loved and appreciated them.

Creativity is not my strongest point, but with this idea God gave me the details and how to arrange my "Love Breakfast."

The breakfast was scheduled for February 14, Valentine's Day, at 10 a.m. at the parsonage. All of the ladies of the church were invited. The invitations were written on the back of kiddie valentines. The menu was kept very simple—coffee, tea, juice, coffee cake, and doughnuts.

A short devotional was prepared on the theme of love. I tried to convey the idea of how much I appreciated them.

The breakfast was a tremendous success with 14 ladies present. Now we have a "Love Breakfast" once a month based around different themes. This idea can be rearranged to fit almost every situation. I praise God for His idea.

MRS. PETER (NANCY) SCHARLER
Midland, Pennsylvania

A Ministry of Mail

As ministers' wives we can all have a ministry of MAIL. This is a caring ministry. Perhaps it is difficult for us to realize the encouragement and appreciation this act of loving and sharing really brings. Here are a few suggestions.

- Look for ways to send thank-you notes and letters.
- Look for ways to send birthday cards.
- Look for ways to send anniversary cards.
- Look for ways to send get-well letters and cards.
- Look for ways to send a letter of encouragement, concern, or telling a person you are praying for them.
- Look for ways to send a note to a person who comes to your mind while praying (probably God's providence).
- Look for ways to send a note of appreciation for some service that a person has given for your church, community, or family.
- Look for ways to send a note to tell someone how much you appreciate their ministry, special solo, directed a VBS, children's ministry, etc.
- Look for ways to send a note just stating, "So happy you were in our service; please, do come again!"
- Look for ways to send a letter to congratulate people on some family achievement.
- Look for ways to send a letter or a note of encouragement and friendliness to the senior citizens or to the shut-in from your congregation and community.
- Look for ways to write your love and concern to unsaved relatives and friends.
- Look for ways to send a letter or note to encourage and give scripture to a new Christian.

There are so many ways we can use our time and our "Mail Ministry." People can see Jesus' love when we care enough to tell them. Try it, you will enjoy it.

MRS. ARTHUR E. (ARLENE) MOTTRAM
St. Louis, Missouri

Christmas Outreach

As a Christmas gift to the community, we advertise an annual December Free Day-Care Service. Each Saturday from 10 to 4, we turn our fellowship hall into a child-care center for mothers who need to do unencumbered Christmas shopping.

The children register and receive name tags at the door. They are then introduced to the leaders in each area of activity: the *Kitchen Korner* (dolls, dishes, and playhouse toys), two separate *table areas* (coloring books & puzzles for younger children, and table games for older children), an *Action Center* (cars, building blocks, & activity toys), a *Reading Corner,* a *Creativity Corner* with a Christmas project for each child to make (such as tree ornaments out of egg-carton shells), and a *Babyland* with playpen, swing, and small toddler toys for the very young.

A morning and afternoon snack are served after a unified story time, and a hot lunch is provided at noon. The helpers volunteer for two- to four-hour work shifts and usually, each year as the Day Care grows, the mothers volunteer to serve a Saturday shift also in exchange for the use of the convenience on another day. To avoid chaos, set your rules and performance standards in advance, and have them well posted on the walls and/or mimeographed for all workers. Everyone can enjoy the day, if order prevails.

MRS. SAMUEL (ADELE) STORKSON
St. Joseph, Missouri

Fashion Festival

One aspect of our Women's Ministries, and a real outreach in the community, is our Annual Fall Fashion Festival, a style showing revolving around a luncheon in the fall.

We plan a very light menu with basic chicken, potato, and gelatin salads, Ritz crackers, and beverage.

The local shops are cooperative in allowing our men, women, boys, and girls to model their clothing. Coordinating the clothing and contacting the various stores provides a great arm of outreach.

Advertising is important. You can distribute posters in various stores, especially those contributing items for the fashion show. We also find the newspapers cooperative.

Optional items: Taped music, printed programs, tickets to local newspaper photographer, hostesses at entrances and at other locations to assist.

This activity will also stimulate the ladies of the church to work together in coordinating this annual project. Many women will attend who do not attend church anywhere.

Mrs. Dee R. (Diane) Jones
McAllen, Texas

Community Involvement

In September, 1975, Erik and I entered school: He, a shy kindergarten student, and I, a concerned mother. The first "sell" job the school administration did on this mother was to convince me that the PTA needed me.

Frankly, I had reservations; but, after due consideration, I agreed to become a room mother representative. My husband encouraged me in this endeavor, indicating that I needed an outlet away from the church.

Thus began three of the most exciting—and often frustrating, but still rewarding—years I have encountered. What began as an outlet for me has become an outreach for Christ and the church. God has opened doors for personal and public witnessing, such as—prayer and discussion with other room mothers meeting in my home; prayer and scripture sharing before chairing a committee meeting; devotional speaking opportunities at meetings and luncheons; contacts with school faculty members to share Christian resource books; suggestion from a group of teachers to form a Bible study group in my home; prayer partnership with a teacher; counseling with still another teacher who was experiencing the trauma of divorce; and phone calls and special visits from troubled women.

And then there is Carol: I invited her to attend my Sunday school class and, surprise, she came. She returned, again and again. You can imagine my joy as I saw her kneel at the altar and experience God's forgiveness and the spirit of praise I felt when, an appropriate time later, my husband welcomed her into church membership.

Just a concerned mother plus the PTA; but the Holy Spirit has used this combination to reach people for God. "But," you ask, "with church responsibilities do you really have time for PTA?" And I must respond, "With experiences like Carol's, can I afford not to *make* time?"

MRS. MORRIS (YVONNE) CHALFANT
Norwood, Ohio

9

Meditations for Women's Meetings

From Darkness to Light

Pastor Mackety listened patiently as the phone at the Minnesota District parsonage rang several times. He knew it sometimes took Mrs. Bloom a few moments to reach it these days.

"I'm sorry, Brother Mackety," her soft voice answered his request, "my husband isn't in now. Could I help you?"

"I just wanted to report on our American Indian work. I'll call later. But how are you today?"

"Rejoicing in the Lord." Her answer voiced enthusiasm.

"Praise the Lord," Pastor Mackety responded. It was always a blessing to talk with this gracious Christian lady. In spite of her recent affliction, she was spiritually victorious.

"In fact," she continued, "the most wonderful thing happened this morning. I haven't even had a chance to tell my husband, but let me share it with you, if you have the time."

"Do go ahead," he urged. "I'd love to hear it."

"A blind lady, a complete stranger to me, called and said a friend had heard how I recently lost my eyesight and gave her my phone number."

"Well," Pastor Mackety suggested, "probably the friend thought by talking together, you two could share your common problems and encourage each other."

"Yes, I think so," Mrs. Bloom agreed, "but she was very depressed so I listened to her and as opportunity came, I began to tell her what the Lord meant to me. She seemed so hungry for the gospel. Said she'd never heard the way of salvation, so I explained how she could be saved."

"Did she seem receptive?" Pastor Mackety asked.

"Oh, yes, I just led her step by step and she gave her heart to the Lord right there as we prayed over the phone. We wept and rejoiced together. It was wonderful."

Long after putting down the phone, Pastor Mackety found himself humming the words of the songwriter, "Once I was blind, but now I can see, the light of the world is Jesus." Indeed Jesus had come again as prophecy had foretold, "to open their eyes, and to turn them from darkness to light."

MRS. PAUL (EMILY) MOORE
Mount Pleasant, Michigan

Thoughts of a Mother

"Train up a child in the way he should go: and when he is old, he will not depart from it" (Prov. 22:6).

At the beginning of a new year, our minds become conscious of goals for the future. As mothers, we earnestly desire ideals for our children such as the love of nature, its beauty and its mystery; the patriotism that seems almost forgotten in our day; and the awareness and power of Almighty God.

I have jotted down some of the things which I want my children to enjoy:

- Dawn beginning with spires of gold.
- Prismed patterns of frost on a sunlit windowpane.
- The tenderness of infancy.
- Intricate lace of the snowflake.
- Camouflaged goldfinch feasting upon the dandelions.
- Crocuses playing in the snow.
- A renewed promise delivered by the rainbow.
- The sunset curtsying to the stars.
- The boldness of courage.
- Perseverance of the patriots.
- The touch of humor that unlocks the moment of tenseness.
- Inner warmth created by cheering a shut-in.
- Triumph of the soft answer which turned away wrath.
- The wisdom of old age.
- Spontaneity of testimony of newfound faith.
- The miracle of healing.
- The cleanness known only in forgiveness.

- A peace bestowed by the Heavenly Father.
- The calmness of the presence of the Holy Spirit.

These are the legacies I hope for my child.

Mrs. Marvin (Rosalyn) Appleby
Columbia, Kentucky

Garth's God

My new friend Garth was only five years old, and he had never been to church or Sunday school. We were strangers really, but in the secluded atmosphere of my car he decided to share some of his ideas about God. His theology was not too sound, but his thoughts were beautiful and reminded me of a simple truth.

"God is very big," he told me.

I agreed.

"And you know," he continued to inform me, "He is in charge of all life."

"Yes, I know that."

"Not only is He in charge of all life, but He is in charge of the whole world—you know, trees and space and everything. And do you know what?"

"What?"

"He's even in charge of people."

"I know that," I replied. Seeing my opportunity to add a bit of wisdom, I continued, "He really loves us. That's why He sent Jesus."

Not to be outdone, the little theologian continued with his original thought. "God is so big that we can't see Him. He's invisible!"

"Oh!"

"Yes—He's awful big. Do you know why He is invisible?"

"No. Why?"

"'Cuz if people could see Him I think they would want to climb all over Him."

I thought about that as we drove on. Gradually a little boy's insight penetrated my heart. I have to admit that sometimes I have wished I could climb up into the arms of my Heavenly Father and tell Him all about my problems. My little friend knew he wanted to be close to God; this minister's wife feels the same way.

God is big. Bigger than the problems and perplexities of life. Perhaps our theology has become so complicated that we fail to grasp that simple truth.

MRS. RONALD L. (JOAN) WHITTENBERGER
Uhrichsville, Ohio

The First Step

Ethan stretched his 18-month-old body facedown on the kitchen floor and sobbed, "Daddy, Daddy, car." He had wanted to go with Daddy, but Daddy had said No.

Upstairs Mother was gently calling, "Ethan, Ethan, come to Mommy." Again and again she called as she heard him sobbing his way toward her. Finally, he stood in her bedroom doorway, his round face soaked in hot tears. With arms open, his mother called again, "Come to Mommy." He stood firm as though determined to suffer alone. Then he gazed fully into his mother's eyes and lifted one small foot toward her. Before his foot touched the floor she swept him into her arms and held him close.

It is like that with us too. We sob when a loved one leaves us in death. It hurts to want them near and have them gone from us. Still, our Heavenly Father is there. Above our sobs we hear His voice calling, "Come unto Me." Too long we languish alone in our pain.

Our grief seems too great to release. Still His voice calls. We turn our tear-streaked faces and look into His eyes. Before we complete our first step toward Him, He sweeps us into His arms, holding us close. Our chilled lonely heart is warmed. We cling to Him and somehow our grief is less painful. He is there sharing it with us.

Mrs. John E. (Barbara) Borgal
Warwick, New York

Independent Darla

My husband accepted the assignment to sit on a bench and watch Darla while the rest of us shopped in the mall. Before he knew it, our three-year-old granddaughter was missing. Then he spied her on a wall trying to drink from the decorative fountain below.

Grandpa glady would have lifted Darla up for a drink at the nearby fountain if she had only asked. But, the personification of independence, she chose to quench her thirst the hard way.

Self-sufficient Christians who fail to ask the Heavenly Father for help are like that when they come up against difficult situations. We choose the hard way when we disregard Him. He always waits to assist us.

"If any of you lack wisdom, let [her] ask of God, that giveth to all . . . liberally, and upbraideth not; and it shall be given [her]" Jas. 1:5.

Mrs. Russell E. (Pauline) Spray
Lowell, Michigan

What Do You See?

Two people can be in the same circumstances of life. One sees gloom and defeat. The other experiences hope and faith, as Habakkuk did. He sees God at work in circumstances. The Book of Habakkuk in the *Living Bible* offers material for an excellent devotional talk on this subject.

> Hab. 1:5 "Look and be amazed."
> Hab. 2:3 "Just be patient."
> Hab. 3:3 "I see God . . ."
> Conclusion: "What do you see?"

MRS. JAY W. (RUTH) PATTON
Skowhegan, Maine

Furnace or Faith

"For he endured, as seeing him who is invisible" (Heb. 11:27b).

It was a tense moment in Babylon. Because of their loyalty to God, King Nebuchadnezzar had commanded three Hebrew boys cast into the fiery furnace. The onlookers shuddered in horror as the three young men were shoved into the flames. Petrified, the crowd waited for the fire to consume its victims.

Suddenly the king's face portrayed fear and disbelief as he exclaimed, "Did not we throw three men into the fire? Lo, I see four men walking and the fourth one looks like the Son of God!"

God indeed had made himself visible, not only to the Hebrew boys, but also to the king and the onlookers. Many times the invisible God has revealed himself to us. He does not always bring instant delivery from the fiery furnaces; sometimes He climbs in there with us and makes himself visible.

I saw God in the nursery at University Hospital in Oklahoma City, Okla., when the doctors said that only a miracle could save our tiny son. When we thought that we had done all that we could do, God was there. When the car insurance was due and we had no money to pay it, He was there, too. When we prayed for a revival in the local church and the devil tried to defeat us, God was there.

Often Satan focuses our eyes on the furnace rather than on faith. But then, through prayer, our sights are lifted to eternal values. Once more we are able to endure "as seeing him who is invisible" (Heb. 11:27b).

MRS. CHARLES (KAREN) WYLIE
Winfield, Kansas

Cease Useless Striving

Do something! That is our usual tendency in times of crisis or problems. It may be the wrong thing, but it is activity. We comfort ourselves by saying, "At least I'm trying." It takes a great deal of self-discipline to follow the Psalmist's instruction, "Be still and know that I am God" or as the *New American Standard Bible* translates it, "Cease striving and know that I am God" (Ps. 46:10, NASB).

It is harder yet to keep from talking. We feel an urgent need to explain, to interpret, or just rehearse the events. But in Exodus we read, "The Lord will fight for you while you keep silent" (Exod. 14:14, NASB). So not only must we cease our feverish efforts to solve the problem, but we need to stop talking, to quietly but confidently commit it to the Lord, resting in the firm conviction that He knows, and is working for us.

MRS. C. K. (EMMELYNE) HELSEL
Bethany, Oklahoma

Baby Chicks and God's Love

In Luke 13:34, Jesus said, "How often would I have gathered thy children together, as a hen doth gather her brood under her wings, and ye would not!" This beautiful relationship between the mother hen and her chicks is used by our Lord to illustrate His love and care for us.

There are four times when the mother hen calls her chicks to come under her wings. When she finds a bit of food—a crumb, a worm, or a bug—she sounds the dinner call and her babies come running for the dainty morsel.

The mother hen also calls when she sees a black speck in the sky. Then she utters an excited cry and calls the chicks together as protection from the menacing hawk. Again she sounds a danger cluck when she hears the thunder, sees the lightning flash, or feels the cold wind blowing; quickly she sounds her call to summon the baby chicks to shelter from the impending storm. Now at last the sun is set, she quietly calls her little ones to sleep and rest.

God calls like that, too.

MRS. ARTHUR L. (GUYNELL) MULLIS
Columbia, South Carolina

31 Days to a New Prayer Life

Here are 31 prayer lessons for one month based on Andrew Murray's book *With Christ in the School of Prayer.*

1. Lord, teach us to pray—Luke 11:1.
2. In spirit and truth—John 4:23-24.
3. Pray to thy Father, which is in secret—Matt. 6:6.
4. After this manner pray—Matt. 6:9.
5. Ask and it shall be given you—James 4:3, Matt. 7:7-8.
6. How much more—Matt. 7:9-11.
7. How much more the Holy Spirit—Luke 11:13.
8. Because of his importunity—Luke 11:5-8.
9. Pray the Lord of the harvest—Matt. 9:37-38.
10. What wilt thou?—Mark 10:51; Luke 18:41.
11. Believe that ye have received—Mark 11:24.
12. Have faith in God—Mark 11:22-24.
13. Prayer and fasting—Matt. 17:19-21.
14. When ye stand praying, forgive—Mark 11:25.
15. If two agree—Matt. 18:19-20.
16. Speedily, though bearing long—Luke 18:1-8.
17. I know that thou hearest me always—John 11:41-42; Ps. 2:7-8.
18. Whose is this image?—Matt. 22:20; Gen. 1:26.
19. I go unto the Father—John 14:12-13.
20. That the Father may be glorified—John 14:13.
21. If ye abide in me—John 15:7.
22. My words in you—John 15:7.
23. Bear fruit, that the Father may give what ye ask—John 15:16; Jas. 5:16.
24. In my name—John 14:13-14; 16:23-24, 26.
15. At that day—John 16:23-26; Jude 20-21.
26. I have prayed for thee—Luke 22:32; John 16:26; Hebrews 7:25.

27. Father, I will—John 17:24.
28. Father! not what I will—Mark 14:36.
29. If we ask according to His will—1 John 5:14-15.
30. An holy priesthood—1 Pet. 2:5; Isa. 61:6.
31. Pray without ceasing—1 Thess. 5:16-18.

This could be used by a ladies' prayer group for a month of Bible reading and prayer. This book, available in paperback, could be purchased by group members from Nazarene Publishing House.

> MRS. LEON F. (ELIZABETH) WYSS
> *San Diego, California*

Roses and Storms

The wind was blowing. A storm was coming. From my kitchen window, I could see the gray thunderclouds. Across the yard, our neighbor's rose bush was in full bloom with three big roses standing tall. I thought the storm would destroy those roses. Just then a hard rain began falling and the wind was blowing stronger than before. Trees swayed and debris was sweeping down the street and across the yard. But those beautiful, delicate, roses bending with the wind, sprang back to stand tall for the next assault.

I don't know how long I stood there, but just as suddenly as the storm came, it was gone. The sun was shining and everything looked so clean. And those exquisite roses were more beautiful than ever now because all the dust was gone from their petals. The whole bush looked revived.

The Lord spoke to me and said, "Just as those roses weathered the storm, I will help you to weather every storm that comes your way. I will help you to bend—not break!" For when the enemy comes to overwhelm us, we have the assurance that God is with us. "When the enemy shall come in like a flood, the Spirit of the Lord shall lift up a standard against him" (Isa. 59:19).

MRS. DON C. (LYNN) TAYLOR
Booneville, Arkansas

Shepherd of My Life

A few years ago a friend and I were attending a missionary convention and sharing a motel room. We had enjoyed fellowship all evening and now the hour was late. My friend was reading her Bible and as I picked up the Gideon Bible it fell open to a worn, stained page. These were the words I read, "The Lord is my shepherd. I shall not want."

It was very evident that the page had been read often. There was no doubt that some of the dark spots were tearstains. Pictures of many people reading this well beloved passage came to me. There had surely been the sad, lonely, bereaved, and the sinful who had found comfort and forgiveness as they read.

Suddenly I felt great gratitude within me. I was grateful for a trusting shepherd boy who had penned these beautiful words, and also for faithful ones who had introduced me to the Good Shepherd. Today my heart is filled with praise for the One who has led me so tenderly through the years.

"Gentle Shepherd, thank You for Your loving care. You have led me through pleasant places and also through dangerous ones. You have promised to be with me always, even through the valley of death. Grant it Lord, that I shall make it safely through and dwell in Your house forever."

MRS. G. W. (JEANETTE) SHOWS
Nashville, Tennessee

"How?" Not "Why?"

A difficult lesson I'm learning is not to ask, "Why, Lord," but instead "How, Lord?" I recently heard a beautiful illustration of this.

When the angel Gabriel came to Mary to announce the birth of Jesus, she did not ask, *"Why?* Why me, Lord? I can never explain this to Joseph! What will this do to my reputation?"

Instead she asked, *"How* can this be?" The answer was that the Holy Spirit would overshadow her and bring it about. And Gabriel added, "For nothing is impossible with God." Mary's response was total submission.

Problems can overwhelm us: wayward children, tensions in the home or in the church, financial pressures, illness. Our human reaction is to ask *why,* and to try to place blame. But the secret is to ask *how.* How can I respond, react, or change in order to deal with this problem? The answer is always in our total submission, our acceptance. Submission must be to the Holy Spirit before we can even talk about submission to anyone else.

Lord, give me the grace to withdraw the *why* and ask the *how.*

MRS. B. EDGAR (KATHRYN) JOHNSON
Kansas City, Missouri

Have You Seen Them?

Have you seen, anywhere, a tall little lad
And a winsome wee lass of four?
It was only today, barefooted and brown,
That they played by my kitchen door.

It was only today (or maybe a year;
  It could not be twenty, I know)
They were shouting for me to help in their game,
  But I was too busy to go;
Too busy with sweeping and dusting to play—
And now they have silently wandered away.

If by chance you hear of a slim little lad
  And a small winsome lass of four,
I pray you, tell me! To find them again
  I would journey the wide world o'er.

Somewhere, I am sure, they'll be playing a game,
  And should they be calling for me
To come out and help, oh, tell them, I beg,
  I'm coming as fast as can be!
For there's never a house might hold me today
Could I hear the call for me to share in their play.
                    —Author unknown

>   Mrs. Jerry D. (Carolyn) Cordell
>   Redding, California

If You Love People, Tell Them

Vladimir Horowitz, the noted pianist, has said that if he had a fault it was his need to be loved. He did not need people to tell him he played beautifully. He knew if he did or did not. To be loved is the need of every human being. When told, spirits are lifted.

Love can be expressed in many ways. A friendly phone call, an unexpected card or note in the mail, a small gift for no apparent reason except to say, "I like you."

The older people of our day can be lonely in a crowd, even in a church service. After a very active life, many feel they have been placed on a shelf of uselessness. To let them know they are not forgotten can bring cheer and an uplift to a discouraged soul.

Have you brought sunshine into someone's life today? Next Sunday, smile and give an encouraging greeting to an older person in your church—and notice the happiness within your own heart.

MRS. NORMAN R. (LINNEA) OKE
Colorado Springs, Colorado

We Are His Responsibility

Phil. 4:6-7

"Do not be anxious about anything, but in everything, by prayer and petition, with thanksgiving, present your requests to God" (Phil. 4:6-7, NIV).

Andrew Murray said, "God is ready to assume full responsibility for the life wholly yielded to Him."

God wants us to let Him be responsible for every detail of our lives, the little ones as well as the big ones. Sometimes it is easier to let Him have our big problems or burdens than to give him the little problems and let Him work out the smallest detail of our lives. Ps. 37:7 (TLB) reads, "Rest in the Lord; wait patiently for Him to act." In Exod. 14:14 (TLB) we read that the Lord will fight for you and you won't need to lift a finger. Let's not fill our hours with inner anxieties and awful worry. Let's not become unnerved with fears and cares. God wants to accomplish much through us and He will if we will relax in Him and be wholly yielded to Him.

We can then know "the peace of God, which transcends all understanding," and it, "will guard your hearts and your minds in Christ Jesus" (Phil. 4:7, NIV).

MRS. BOB (IDA MAE) MICKEY
Lamar, Colorado